WHAT IS PROGRESS

Aldo Schiavone

WHAT IS PROGRESS

*Translated from the Italian
by Ann Goldstein*

Europa
editions

Europa Editions
1 Penn Plaza, Suite 6282
New York, N.Y. 10019
www.europaeditions.com
info@europaeditions.com

Library of Congress Cataloging in Publication Data is available
ISBN 978-1-60945-668-9

Schiavone, Aldo
What is Progress

Book design by Emanuele Ragnisco
www.mekkanografici.com

Cover illustration by Ginevra Rapisardi

Prepress by Grafica Punto Print – Rome

Printed in the USA

CONTENTS

WHAT IS PROGRESS

THE UNEXPECTED . . .

This short book was finished, and was waiting only to be printed, when the health crisis linked to the spread of Covid-19 emerged in China, and then in Italy and the rest of the world.

I didn't think I needed to change what I had written or add to it. Rather, it seemed to me that events fully confirmed the interpretation I had outlined, and gave it an urgency that I would happily have done without.

I did think it would be useful, however, to include a brief afterword, in which the reader can find stated, more directly and explicitly, my arguments against certain opinions concerning our relationship with nature and with history that, today more than ever, are gaining credibility.

Rome, April 2020

I
THE ANGEL'S GAZE

Let's begin with a familiar passage—at least among those who have some knowledge of art or philosophy—that, as an authentic icon of twentieth-century thought, has been endlessly discussed by the interpreters:

A Klee painting named *Angelus Novus* shows an angel looking as though he is about to move away from something he is fixedly contemplating. His eyes are staring, his mouth is open, his wings are spread. This is how one pictures the angel of history. His face is turned toward the past. Where we perceive a chain of events, he sees one single catastrophe which keeps piling wreckage upon wreckage and hurls it in front of his feet. The angel would like to stay, awaken the dead, and make whole what has been smashed. But a storm is blowing from Paradise; it has got caught in his wings with such violence that the angel can no longer close them. This storm irresistibly propels him into the future to which his back is turned, while the pile of debris before him grows skyward. This storm is what we call progress.

Walter Benjamin (the words are his, written in early 1940, when death was imminent)[1] nurtured a real passion for the small painting he's talking about, which was made by Klee using a technique he invented, combining oil and watercolor. Benjamin had found it, and bought it, in Munich, where he had gone to visit his friend Gershom Scholem, in the spring of 1921, before the artist became famous; and from then on, during the many moves of his tumultuous, battered life, he always had it with him. Today it's in the Israel Museum in Jerusalem.

The painting also impressed Ernst Bloch, who had seen it in Benjamin's house and wrote about it in the twenties. "Paul Klee sketched a page, *Angelus Novus*; the angel has the horror in front of him, the wind of the future behind," he said,[2] already anticipating the nucleus of Benjamin's interpretation, although it's very possible that Bloch, who later went on to study the idea of progress in detail,[3] was reporting an intuition formulated first by his host.

In any case, the fact is that Benjamin's (or maybe Bloch's, earlier) description rather than explain Klee's image overwhelms it, superimposing the features of a new scene and submerging Klee's—more enigmatic in its suspended drama—in a conceptual and visual order that doesn't belong to it but constitutes, so to speak, a completely free reading, charged with metaphysics. The angel, as protagonist—caught in the act perhaps of an annunciation, or even just a desperate cry—appears now as the impotent target on whom an immense, irresistible force is exerted, and revealed as the genuine focus of the new vision. He wants to oppose it, but can't. The fury of the tempest that rages all around gives him no respite; it's a whirlwind that the gaze can't penetrate. The past, history, on which his unveiled eyes, not deluded by the false perspectives of men, are fixed, is an unsalvageable pile of ruins, reaching up to heaven. Progress—the idea that Benjamin saw disastrously refuted—was the uninterrupted rush of the catastrophe toward the inscrutable heart of the storm. It wasn't completely negated: the forward movement continued, unstoppable; but it was reduced to the storm's pure, naked violence, waiting for a redemption—or at least a meaning—that didn't arrive.

For Benjamin what emerged fully in this picture was a kind of quintessence of the twentieth century: velocity and tragedy, power and the unknown, metaphysics and destiny. "Progress"—the word, inherited from nineteenth-century thought, was still familiar and full of promise—had become an endless, useless flight dragging us inexorably through an ocean of ruins: no one knew where, or even if a where existed and was humanly discernible.

Eighty years later, the state of mind to which Benjamin lent such an agitated and absorbing representation seems to have become—if in a more tenuous and softened form—an inevitable companion of our unsettled days, even though the conditions, at least in the West, are much less violent than those which affected Benjamin's life (and death). In fact, it seems like the tonality of an era, not the faint reverberation of a distant past of anguish and devastation.

In the interval that separates us from that era, a clarifying light has returned only intermittently, while the mere thought of progress becomes steadily and desolately outmoded, to the point where the word itself is unutterable: a flag transformed into a sign of irrevocable disappointment, not to say deception and betrayal. It's as if our sense and view of the future, and the very meaning of history, had been definitively swallowed up by an indissoluble lump of pessimism, bewilderment, and uncertainty; and the present—unmoving and shut up in itself, in an opaque, fictitious eternity—were our only refuge.

What happened to plunge us into this swamp of unassuageable bad feeling?

The answer isn't simple, but it will carry us far.

Modernity, from the Renaissance on—the "new age" of Europe's path—was constructed around very different attitudes. It was based on the conviction that the ceaseless activity of human beings—the productivity of their effort, their intelligence, their daily labor—was creating the foundation for a continual change for the better in our modes of life, at least in the part of the world that Europeans inhabited: a privileged region (it was thought), called on to build a civilization without equal that would elaborate standards and rules to be imposed in the four corners of the earth.[4]

The changes evoked were not only material; the transformation would also include a refinement in the capacities for evaluation and discernment, and for moral judgment itself—that is, minds, too, would become "enlightened," stronger and more penetrating, on the way to an increasingly successful civilization.

This widespread faith went along with a new vision— both philosophical and theological—of time and history, developed during the course of modernity: a turning point that analyses of the past century insisted on, not without some exaggeration and strain. The ancient con cept of a circular and repetitive temporality—the idea of history as a cycle, of an immutable and "natural" repetition of the chain of events: the myth of the Eternal Return—was replaced by the properly Christian interpretation of linear time, with a beginning and an end, marked by the incarnation of the Son of God, and by the achievement of his eschatological project of redemption and salvation.

It's also true that in a remarkable comment,[5] confined with unmatched (and perhaps unconscious) nonchalance to a very long footnote, Santo Mazzarino, one of the great classical scholars of the twentieth century, demonstrated conclusively that an opposition so unequivocal couldn't be sustained, and that the two images—the circle and the line, ancient and modern— were in reality much more closely entwined, overlapping

and intersecting: and there is little to add to this recon-
struction. Nevertheless, it's undeniable that the empha-
sis on the direction of time—on the existence of a vector
of history, so to speak—belonged specifically to the
character of Western modernity, and, starting with the
culture of the Renaissance, was paired with the development of a fundamentally optimistic idea of the relationship between past and future.

The golden age was ahead of us, not behind, as the
ancients believed; and we could and should reach it,
even if at the end of a difficult and unknowable journey.
The effects of the first technological gains of the new era
(ocean navigation, firearms, printing) contributed significantly to this conviction, along with the change in the
paradigms of natural history (both cosmological and
geological) and, above all, the discovery of the evolutionary path of the earth, regarding which Thomas
Burnett, as early as 1680 or 1690, used the term
"progress,"[6] while James Hutton, a century later, discovered the unfathomable—even if uniform, according to
him—span of its geologic eras.[7]

Anyway, not until the eighteenth and nineteenth centuries, starting with, let's say, the Age of Enlightenment,
did the word "progress" and the idea that it represented
become common in the West. In the *Essay on Universal
History, the Manners, and Spirit of Nations*, published in
1756, Voltaire had written:

Based on the picture we've traced of Europe from

the time of Charlemagne to our days it's easy to judge how this part of the world is incomparably more populated, more civilized, wealthier, more enlightened than it was then, and that it is also much superior to what was the Roman Empire, excluding Italy.[8]

These reflections were certainly known to Edward Gibbon when he formulated his famous comparison, at the start of *The Decline and Fall of the Roman Empire*, in which, deliberately provocative, he declared that the splendor of the age of the Antonines was destined to remain without equal on the path of humanity.[9] The statement soon became the canon of a true historiographical stereotype, which made the present an obligatory standard of comparison by which to judge the past. Likewise these reflections were certainly known to Madame de Staël, writing *De la Littérature*, which, published in 1800, was constructed entirely on the idea of happy and uninterrupted progress in the field of letters.[10]

The nineteenth century was thus preparing to become "the great century of the idea of progress" (as Jacques Le Goff writes in a fine essay).[11] François Guizot, in his *Cours d'histoire moderne*, of 1829, had associated with the notion the very idea of civilization: "It seems to me that the idea of progress . . . is the fundamental idea contained in the word 'civilization.'"[12]

Along those lines, and at around the same time, came the much more powerful structure of Hegel's philosophy, with its interweaving of logic and meta-physics based entirely on the primacy of the present with respect to any period of the past ("reason is the present").[13] This motif was adopted variously by all historicist trends, from those of romantic inspiration (in the history of law, literature, language) to Hegelian and, later, Marxist tendencies, and then Dilthey and Italian idealism; and by Marx, who was closely connected to Hegel on this point as well (the present explains the past and not vice versa: human anatomy is a key to the anatomy of the ape, and not the contrary, according to the famous aphorism formulated at the culmination of the 1857 Introduction to *A Contribution to the Critique of Political Economy*).[14]

The long positivist era contributed as much as the different versions of historicism to the success of the idea, in an especially significant convergence: we have only to think of Comte and his *Cours de philosophie positive*, published between 1830 and 1842.[15] And in French culture early socialist thought also played a role in the dissemination of this concept of progress: in 1839, Louis Blanc had founded the *Revue du progrès,* and in 1853 Proudhon wrote the *Philosophie du progrès.*[16]

In England, on the other hand, it was mainly evolutionary theories, with Spencer (*Principles of Psychology* came out in 1855)[17] and Darwin (*On the Origin of Species* appeared in 1859),[18] that encouraged a progressive paradigm to take root, although it was formulated with a different perspective—less philosophical and oriented more toward the natural sciences—from the French, German, and, later, Italian versions.

Thus an essentially uniform portrait was composed. Everywhere in Europe, the movement of great revolutions in technology, economy, and politics—steam engines, capitalist production, and the laissez-faire model—was concentrated in the shared vision that made progress the engine of history, however you wanted to imagine it. And faith in what it expressed—that humanity, or at least the avant-garde, was on an irresistible forward march—looked better and better as the ideology of an entire era in Western history: as the background of an age that triggered a sequence of transformations in ways of life such as humanity had never known before. (These were enthusiastically celebrated in the London Exposition of 1851: an impassioned apologia for industrialization that, designing the new face of imperial England, was pushing the whole world forward and upward.)

In fact, the changes that took place had a truly unparalleled reach, allowing the historian David Landes[19] to maintain, retrospectively, and with good reason, that the material conditions of an English gentleman's life in the mid-eighteenth century were more like those of a legionnaire of Caesar than like those of his great-grandchildren. Less than a century created a greater distance than almost two millennia had.

Acceleration had become the sign of the times par excellence, and enabled astonishing comparisons between past and present: comparisons that fueled in particular the idea of progress, whose diffusion was a direct consequence of this new and unprecedented velocity.

The history of Europe thus appeared to be the narrative—familiar to all far beyond Voltaire's first statements—of an unstoppable journey that at every stage was preparing for a future of further inevitable gains, to the point where "the unification of mankind" (thus Prince Albert, the husband of Queen Victoria, in 1851)[20] could be imagined, or "the decisive advent of a new spiritual power" (as Comte wrote in 1848).[21] It was a mental climate that lasted until the early years of the next century, at least until the fatal August, 1914, and the battlefields of the Marne and Verdun.

In giving increasing support to this point of view, nineteenth-century European and American culture (and not only the facets directly attributable to positivism) emphasized, as we've already hinted, a particular feature. The center was being shifted from the historical and literary field to the technological and scientific axis. In truth, this shift was already perceptible in Condorcet and, on another level, had been perfectly clear in the general mind-set of the young United States, even at its less cultured levels—at least as it appeared to Tocqueville's[22] attentive gaze—ever since the American Revolution. In that sense, an anecdote he recounts in *Democracy in America* is truly memorable: the story of the sailor who considered it pointless to build ships whose structures would endure through time, because surely they would soon be replaced by vastly improved ships. It describes the nascent state of an attitude and a way of thinking that led to the rosy industrialist visions of Henry Ford and Frederick Taylor, and the birth of the "American dream."

Progress thus became first of all advances in the knowledge of nature and the consequent technological attainments. The century that had begun with sailboats and candles ended with the great transatlantic liners, transcontinental railroads, telegraph wires on the bottom of the ocean, cars, the telephone, electricity. Nothing similar had ever occurred in the history of the planet, and it seemed impossible not to take proper account of it. Inventions and discoveries were no longer distant, isolated events but a single continuous, exciting process: technology bred technology, in an uninterrupted succession that conditioned production and the market, pushing the latter to finance further innovations with increasing prodigality, in a fugue without end.

A book like Colin Clark's *The Conditions of Economic Progress*,[23] of 1940, reflects clearly, and even a little late, this shift in the concept of progress toward science and technology (even though in the twentieth century English-language economists soon began replacing the word "progress" with what was, in their judgment, the less demanding and more neutral word "growth").

But it would certainly be a mistake to reduce all nineteenth-century thought to the terms just described.

In its unfolding we can easily find very different accents, even if they are often irreconcilable, and united only by a common rejection of that trusting expectation of the marvels of the future that was becoming the spirit of the age, an almost untouchable idol: from Leopardi to Nietzsche, for example (the philosopher read the Italian poet: he had some translations in his library, and had even paraphrased in German *Saturday in the Village*).[24] Not to mention Kierkegaard and Schopenhauer, or what we could define as the romantic-irrational genre of criticism directed at the scientific intellect, developed mainly in England, in relation to the achievements of mechanism and industrial scientism: from Mary Shelley's *Frankenstein* to Robert Louis Stevenson's *Strange Case of Dr. Jekyll and Mr. Hyde* and Bram Stoker's *Dracula*.

Or, on the more straightforwardly political front, openly reactionary culture (*réaction* was the word used by Charles Maurras, in 1899, in *Action française,* an ideological manifesto of the extreme right in France): ranging from a bitter, early enemy of the Revolution like the Savoyard Joseph De Maistre to the racist rants of Arthur de Gobineau (*Essai sur l'inégalité des races humaines,* [*Essay on the inequality of the human races*], is from 1853-55),[25] down to (and we are on yet another level) the Catholic positions expressed in the eighty propositions of the *Syllabus*—commissioned by Pius IX in 1864—the last of which considered inadmissible a judgment that "the Roman Pontiff can, and ought to, reconcile himself, and come to terms with progress, liberalism, and modern civilization."[26]

But it was still a matter of relatively isolated voices, including that Catholic intransigence: the latter in particular was soon reduced to the feelings of a minority, albeit fierce, within the Church of Rome. Such attitudes never got to the point of overturning the course of the dominant intellectual currents, or of forming a true alternative common feeling, at least in the more important segments of public opinion: urban masses, professional and productive middle classes, political élites.

The twentieth century, in turn, with the dizzying increase in the rhythm of change that we've just noted, put an even stronger accent on science and technology, now heavily involved in the idea of progress. The tempo of change began to be measured not in centuries or fifty-year periods but in rapid decades. The thirties were not comparable to the years of the Belle Époque: people flew regularly (in planes and in dirigibles); listened to the radio; were treated with sulfa drugs. And they were not comparable to the fifties, with television, atomic weapons, jets, antibiotics, plastic, transistors; or the seventies, with transplants, electronics, lunar exploration, and telecommunication satellites. Not to mention the last twenty years of the century, which saw, with the decline of the mechanical and chemical industries in the advanced countries, nanotechnologies, information technology, the internet, cell phones, the beginnings of bioengineering. In short, the vertigo of an endless race.[27]

*

And yet, almost suddenly, something began to go wrong with progress, something profound began to eat into the solidity of the conviction. Some books that appeared in the middle decades of the century, mostly in France, offer eloquent testimony regarding this abrupt change of atmosphere. In 1936, Georges Friedmann—a prominent scholar who was among the founders of the sociology of work in Europe—published a penetrating essay, entitled *La crise du progrès. Esquisse d'histoire des idées: 1895-1935*:[28] an unthinkable choice before 1914. (In fact, as early as 1908 Georges Sorel had written *Les illusions du progrès*,[29] but it was a weak and superficial critique, the product of a Marxism that was mannered and full of misinterpretations, such as that espoused by the philosopher in his youthful years; it didn't touch on any really essential issues and had no appreciable echo, either political or cultural.)

Thus arose a series of interpretations that, despite the many differences among them, ended up at Raymond Aron and his *Les désillusions du progrès. Essai sur la dialectique de la modernité*, which appeared much later, in 1969.[30] And the work of John Bagnell Bury, *The Idea of Progress. An Inquiry Into Its Origin and Growth*,[31] of 1920, while far from hostile toward the concept it was examining, still kept its distance, accepting it only with reservations and conditionally.

The excitement of the nineteenth century was now at least scaled down, and it never revived. Of course, the

West's technological store (and after 1867 that of Japan as well, which was now in full, extremely rapid industrial and capitalist flight) continued to grow: that was undeniable. But, at the same time, the twentieth century, with its fitful, disjointed advance, was demonstrating a dark, stormy side that through the early years of the century— still overflowing with optimism—seemed absolutely unexpected.

First, there was the tremendous shock of the war, which broke out when it could least have been predicted, and was an atrocious slaughter. The unthinkable suddenly became reality, while the hopes of the Belle Époque were shattered by the fury of the European conflict, which turned into a devastating world clash. This was soon followed by an even more murderous repeat, which led to the horror of the Shoah, an event whose appalling dimensions became more evident with the years, the crushing layers of evidence, and the voices of the survivors: a mass annihilation of the human made possible by the self-annihilation of consciences in the heart of Europe. This laceration could not be repaired or redeemed, and provoked the sensation, if not always explicit, of an indelible original sin. It was the ultimate end of human ingenuity, which drew in all of modernity and tore forever the fabric of the time that had produced it into a "before" and an "after" that couldn't be rejoined.

Was this inconceivable horror—prophetically intuited by Benjamin in the eyes of Klee's angel—the progress that was so vaunted? And then wasn't Leopardi's sarcasm perhaps the more justified when, defeated among the defeated in the desolation of Italy, he desperately mocked "magnificent, progressive destiny"?[32]

Nor did it help to look away from that destruction, to turn aside from the tragedies of the double war and consider only the economic and social aspects, the widespread improvement in the quality of life: the severity of the crisis of 1929, in Europe and America, had swept away every illusion about the miraculous virtues of industrialization and the capitalist market and the more or less equal distribution of advantages that would inevitably derive from it. And wasn't the peace itself—at what cost achieved, after 1945—immediately transformed into a hugely risky, precarious equilibrium on the edge of an abyss, always a step away from the possibility of a nuclear catastrophe that could compromise even the survival of life on our planet?

As the century advanced, following the thread of what appeared to be a paradox but in reality obeying the rhythms of a strict causality, a surprising symmetry established itself. While the conditions of life improved, thanks to the increase in technological achievements, the perception that history was on a reassuring path, encouraging expectations that times would inevitably get better, seemed to waver and fade, if not disappear completely.

That conviction had been too fiercely refuted to be offered again as a credible anchor. Despite the unquestionable gains of science—in part, precisely because of them—the horizon was filled with shadows and the way forward confusingly twisted. Perhaps Heidegger's ideas could best present, for the first half of the twentieth century (and later, in Italy, Emanuele Severino's), the darkening horizons and consequent dramatic distance from an indiscriminate trust in the scientific attainments of the new times. Technology announced not redemption but condemnation. The old positivist optimism was turned upside down, exposing an extremely delicate nerve in the very heart of modernity.

The contradiction was profound. The condensation, crystallization, and diffusion of the first nuclei, especially European ones, of "negative thought" on the meaning of history—thought that was harshly critical of the idea of progress—revealed a problem of the West that was even more severe than the wounds produced by the two world wars. The twentieth century was the longest, densest, and most complex in the history of the world—not the "short century," as Eric Hobsbawm[33] later called it, in an analysis in other ways stimulating.

We can perceive this contrast—starting in the seventies but noticeable earlier—in the devastating, increasingly visible, and destabilizing dissociation between the pace of technological advances, on the one hand, and, on the other, the struggle or incapacity of the rest of human history to adapt positively. The split was, with ups and downs, present throughout the past century, and in the first two decades of this one, mainly after the economic crisis of 2008, reached its most acute and critical point so far.

The division not only saw the rapid accumulation of technological and scientific developments and their transformative projection into the reality of every individual life; it also witnessed the corresponding and increasing difficulty of producing a cultural and social plan and a political and governmental rationality—in the geopolitical order and in the individual nations—adequate to the scenarios that were taking shape. And all this was happening precisely when there was an even greater need to keep up with the onslaught of changes, and control and master them for the best.

Or, in other words, if we want to use a shorter, more synthetic formula: the growing imbalance between power (technological), on one side, now capable, in more ways than one, of destroying the planet itself, and rationality (civil and political) on the other; between the capacity of technology and the capitalist economy to foster not only innovation, wealth, and opportunity but, at the same time, unprecedented dangers and dissymmetries—that is, to intensify the ambivalent character of these potentialities—and the corresponding incapacity to guide the processes according to rational global choices. That is, to guide them toward goals that are not merely the maximization of profits and the unrestrained satisfaction of particular interests, whether political or economic, national or class.

The most severe crisis concerning the idea of progress was generated entirely—it seems to me—by the trauma caused by that fracture: by the structural, systemic imbalance between power and reason, and an awareness of the extreme difficulty of resolving it. This split, in a way anticipated by the world wars, was manifested more clearly during the Cold War and became glaringly obvious after the technological revolution at the end of the twentieth century.

In the American sensibility the perception of this failure advanced in an intricate and complex way, related to ingrained characteristics of the culture. The twentieth century was also the American century, in which the power of the United States radiated throughout the world. It was a matter not only of military might—itself without precedent—or of purely economic supremacy, which was in any case uncontainable, but of the capacity to impose as successful and desirable a style of consumption and life such as had never been seen before; to make technological innovation a continuous process, based on an uninterrupted flow of transformative inventions immediately employed in industrial production; to set forth as exemplary a model of society that was flexible, open, and inclusive—far from the locked-in classes of the old European countries—in spite of the indelible stain of slavery and its consequences, which continue to manifest themselves; to establish and maintain a democracy as a "complete social fact" and not only as a formal system; to develop a culture able, through music and literature, to speak to the world, and in particular to the world of the young. In a word: to have made the "American dream" a universal dream.

That primacy, however, had not acquired the characteristics of what is traditionally called an "empire," in the meaning that it had in the past when referring to Spain and England and their colonial lands; or to indicate the possessions of Rome in its thousand-year history. (Besides, "empire" was a word that for a long time American culture—even the most watchful and critical with respect to its own politics—obstinately refused to accept concerning the country's supremacy, in a curious correspondence with ancient Rome, where *imperium* meant something entirely different, and no word existed to indicate in a distinct and unitary way the conquered territories.)

Rather, for the United States it was the conscious exercise of a complete transoceanic hegemony, in the most precise, Gramscian sense of the term. This hegemony has been able, so to speak, to globalize the West—especially in the last twenty years of the twentieth century, when it seemed increasingly clear that Communism had lost the game forever. It was something similar to an imperial attitude, if we can call it that—but without the actuality of an empire—in which economic and military superiority, while present and visible in the background, was constantly refashioned in the terms of a network of international relations formally egalitarian but intrinsically and substantially asymmetrical. And it had an overall scientific and cultural primacy—transmitted by the worldwide diffusion of English—that was able to give shape to an entire civilization.

Thus the principal nucleus of what we might call the American ideology—the ideology of American preeminence in the twentieth century—materialized. And in that construction faith in progress—the same described magisterially by Tocqueville in a prophetic passage on the essence of the American soul—continued to play an essential role. That is, the conviction that the history of the United States had to be a path inevitably oriented toward a linear increase in freedom, wealth, well-being, and power, projected beneficently onto the entire world.

The European tragedies—the Shoah, the two civil wars—ultimately appeared blurry and distant in that vision: ghosts of a world that vanished on the beaches of Normandy in June, 1944. Of course, sometimes interruptions and gaps were created in that faith, cracks that let doubts and bad feelings creep in: the intervention in Vietnam—the end of American innocence, it has been said—and the youth protests of the late nineteen-sixties were undoubtedly significant examples. But the basic outline of the progressive concept—which not even the crash of 1929 or the worst moments of the Cold War had managed to shatter—was always able to endure and renew itself, thanks in part to the two waves represented first by the Roosevelt New Deal and then, after the war, by Kennedy and the image of the New Frontier.

And when, in 1989, the Soviet Union collapsed conclusively, and some thought that, even if what was happening wasn't the end of history, it could at least be considered the end of the great contradictions of history, it was still in reality the original idea of progress speaking, now directly coinciding with the very future of the planet.

It was only with the start of the new century that the picture began to darken: after September 11th, and then after the economic crisis of 2008, it appeared evident, somewhat surprisingly, that not everything that was happening could be brought within the framework of a continuous increase in opportunity and hope, and that the global world was also a complex and difficult place for the superpower that had contributed decisively to creating it. The Trump years have been the unequivocal sign of a disorientation and an apprehension that distanced America from much of the optimism that characterized its past.

As for Western Europe, however, as long as Marxist thought and the imposing ideological-political apparatus based on it in some sense lasted, their hold served as a barrier to the widespread and heightened distrust of the time that was supposed to come. Although that paradigm was far from any mechanically deterministic interpretation of Marxist theory, it was based on setting up and maintaining a positive relationship with the future, along with a progressive dynamic between past, present, and future that had won over enormous masses, for entire generations, filling the horizon of their ideas with hope. However one thought of constructing Communism, faith in it necessitated, after all, a belief that, even amid countless difficulties, history tended toward increasingly evolved social forms and, in the final analysis, betterment. It was only a matter of fighting to create the conditions of the most rapid and efficient transition that could be achieved in the given circumstances. It wasn't nothing: one had to keep in mind that at every stage unforeseen events could happen and launch scenarios full of unsuspected variations; yet there was no doubt that the entire process had a positive stamp.

But, with the conclusive decline of that perspective, which, with the events of the last decade of the twentieth century, had become merely "the passing of an illusion" (to use the words of an important if painful book by François Furet),[34] the last defense also failed. The collapse of Communism squandered the greatest, most elaborate investment in the overall progressive meaning of history deployed by thought in the nineteenth and twentieth centuries and perhaps in all of human experience: a conceptual and ideological scaffolding that had had incalculable effects, changing the lives of hundreds of millions of women and men throughout the world. The collapse of that structure left everyone—including its stubborn adversaries—more defenseless and more alone.

Furthermore, the loss had another, no less important effect. The world became a place where what we had become accustomed to for most of the twentieth century no longer existed: alternative systems, radically opposed models—on the one hand Western societies, on the other socialist—whose forced coexistence nevertheless generated rules and symmetry, however strained by the continuous risk of military clashes. From the moment of the capitalist triumph, it was as if the great dialectic had abandoned the theater of history, surrendering its contradictions to a one-dimensionality that seems to shrink and impoverish the range of possibilities that we used to attribute to the future. And yet it didn't reduce the new divisions and unprecedented conflicts created by that victory, and no one is worrying about providing a way out that does not exacerbate the wounds and lacerations. It's as if we had been abandoned to a world of contradictions, but without the hope of dialectic, of overcoming the negative.

After the Second World War, and during the so-called Cold War, there were in fact intervals when it seemed that we might have been able to look toward the future again with greater control and optimism, and that the clash between East and West, between capitalist countries and socialist regimes, could be resolved not in a nuclear holocaust but in something like an advanced synthesis, or at least a mutual, positive blend—and thus in a general improvement in people's lives—thanks to prolonged peaceful coexistence.

The nineteen-seventies and eighties, for example, had on several occasions seen a succession of such expectations, which, in the West, involved broader experiences of the politics of welfare and the "third way," between free-market capitalism and "real social-ism" (as it was called at the time). These were periods during which, it seemed, the word "progress" could be uttered again almost everywhere, and continuing tech-nological advances (the space race, the first develop-ments of computer science and telecommunications satellites, discoveries in the field of biology) seemed to make the vision of a gradual transformation not only possible but closer: progress, precisely, toward a world more humane, balanced, and livable.

But history loves abrupt changes of pace, leaps, unexpected mutations; even if humans, in an effort to soothe themselves, almost always try to reduce its image to the deceptive measure of a regular, uninterrupted flow, where everything happens slowly, "step by step" (that's how it is in almost all historicism). And a sudden change of scenario—predicted by no one—was precisely what once again awaited us.

The last stretch of the twentieth century saw one of the most important breaks (if not the most significant absolutely) in the modern era: the start of the third tech-nological revolution in human history, after the agricul-tural and the industrial, and the consequent emergence from the age of the great factory systems and the form of work connected to them, mass labor; and, along with this change, the unexpected collapse of the Soviet empire and the Communist regimes of Eastern Europe.

The two series of events, both of incalculable reach, were much more closely related than they appeared in the mirror of contemporary chronicles and the early, not very enlightening historical investigations.

Almost overnight, the social and political landscape of the entire planet changed. And the technological leap—which, by nineteenth-century measures, should have seemed the ultimate confirmation of the validity of the idea of progress—in the end provoked a new, even more serious wave of anxiety and bewilderment, because it accentuated with incomparably greater force the very gap we're talking about between the speed of technology and the capacity of the rest of history to keep up in a comprehensively rational way.

The world that emerged from the transformation— the one before us today—is undoubtedly much more unified and interdependent than before, at least where the great urban areas, on all continents, are concerned: globalized by goods, by consumption (including cultural: music, fashion, communications), by the sharing of technologies and the tendential uniformity of life styles, especially among the young. And the fluidity and intensity of contacts certainly spread benefits and multiply opportunities, even for entire peoples who never enjoyed them before and have made their entrance into history, so to speak—in China for example.

But from the point of view of the social conflicts and tensions that have emerged in various countries and in international relations—from the point of view of the world order, of the human capacity to govern globally an increasingly integrated and therefore more fragile and vulnerable reality—the scene has become much more lopsided, fragmented, and chaotic.

The victory of capital has unified the planet. And yet it has also reset the laboriously won perception of the historicity of capitalist economic forms (repeating to a certain extent what happened before Marxism), making them appear natural and eternal again (which is what occurred at the start of the nineteenth century), so that all depth is removed from our perspective and our gaze is blocked, as before an insurmountable barrier. It's as if capitalist rationality had to coincide totally and seamlessly with human rationality, in an apparently impermeable overlay that produces tensions, conflicts, unfulfilled needs for governability and for realistic and practical alternatives.

To confront this situation, and resolve the imbalance, a great intellectual and political effort is needed, similar to what was achieved by Marxism and the reform movements of the nineteenth and twentieth centuries in Europe and America, and capable of cancelling the effects of this deviation. It has to design a political and ethical form of the world that can support the weight of technological development and project it indefinitely into the future, past the thick hedge that is hiding from us what is to come.

Nothing like that has happened so far.

Of course, the separation of the most important

structures of production from their old national config-
urations, rooted in a single territory (a past now conclusively lost), the dematerialization of many of their
processes, the increasingly tight network of financial
streams and technological innovations, and the daily
experience of the unrestricted movements of people,
capital, and ideas—this combination of elements is creating, for those inside the fluid, expansive, incandescent
bubble produced by them, unexplored relationships
and attitudes. That is, a kind of nascent state for a new
dimension of life in which dynamics and opportunities
develop that in turn prefigure successive, continuous
transformations.

This explosion of possibilities, however, contains
previously unthinkable risks and conflicts: it multiplies
new inequalities in the heart of the West, creates vast,
unforeseen areas of exclusion, and activates mechanisms
of discrimination thought to have been left behind forever, without providing even a glimpse of an antidote. At
the same time, pessimistic predictions of a diametrically
opposed fate are overturning the conviction—so deeply
rooted that it has become a mass conditioned reflex—
that, from one generation to the next, for the great
majority of those living in our countries, there could be
only improvement in social conditions, improvement
that has been, so to speak, the individual and particular
way of experiencing the idea of progress.

That is, this conviction is being transformed into the
idea—widespread now not only among the working

classes but also the old middle and even upper middle classes, especially after the financial collapse of 2008—that we have to fight in order not to fall behind, dig in to defend what we've gained, which now feels threatened and precarious. And we are fueling the impulse to fight this battle in a closed, corporate way, considering anyone who doesn't belong to our own circle an enemy, confusing the identity of the culture and history of an entire country with the protection of a small personal space of self-consciousness: the only thing to safeguard when we are convinced that the prospect for positive change is reduced to a remote probability and, realistically, can no longer be counted on.

If we add to all this the ever greater knowledge of the damage that can be done and is already being done to the planet's ecological equilibrium, if global politics and the global economy don't immediately assume (though it's still not clear how) the preservation of the environment and natural resources as a primary, non-negotiable value, to defend not by rejecting technology but by intensifying its benign use, the darkness of the portrait is completed in an even more disquieting way.

In place of a renewed faith in progress, a true future syndrome is saturating our era. The perception of the lack of culture and government we were talking about has been transformed into something close to a true state of suffering, with mass dimensions. The shadow of threats that we perceive as imminent cancels out any careful, objective evaluation of the results achieved and the journey just completed. Fleeing into the present—an omnivorous present, immeasurably expanded, which doesn't recognize anything behind it or ahead—appears to be the only response that can in some way calm unease. And politics doesn't help: it, too, has been reduced almost everywhere to a short-term challenge, impoverished in language and ideas, perpetually and narrowly focused on the business of the day; it has become a competition between contenders who not only resemble but increasingly identify with each other in a downward shift, without plans, without talents, without world views, without perspectives that are not the acquisition or the pure and simple conservation of power, here and now—and let the rest wait.

Luckily for us this isn't all there is. In the face of an unease that is more acute every day, a need is growing—strong but so far unmet—for alternatives that would drastically reorient our lives; for a radical break in mental attitude, at least equal to what has marked, in the economy, the technological leap of these decades; for the return of dialectical thinking able to find in the negative the positive germ of the future that awaits us. And it's clear that this turn can't concern only this or that country, this or that social group, but has to be no less global than economic relations, markets, financial streams.

We still don't know exactly which direction to take, what path to follow in order to revive our societies, to imbue them with energy and security—together with the democratic dream of modernity that the twentieth century was able to make universal as never before—and to reconstruct communities worthy of the name, measured by a new, shared equality that can live with difference and the idea of the "other," and not just with individuals dominated by bitterness, fear, and mutual exclusion. We are starting to realize that the times require a new relationship between our species and the planet, between us and life in this corner of the universe, and that to construct it we have to recapture an image of the future for our civilization as a resource and a plan, and stop thinking of it as a lost horizon.

In other words, the angel—the angel of history evoked by Klee and then by Benjamin—has to turn and finally agree to look ahead, into the heart of the storm. And all of us, together, have to look with him.

II
WHERE THE ARROW GOES

Challenged by the weight of the difficulties, the idea of progress, and the state of mind that accompanies its success, emerges weakened if not overwhelmed. It can no longer express anything that truly concerns us.

Is there really no recourse but to admit that, however impressive, the growth in the scientific and technological foundation of our societies—the tremendous leap that we've just begun to experience—isn't enough to set up a different basis on which to judge the present? Is the common perception, then, reliable, not just the result of an error in perspective we need to free ourselves from to see things with greater objectivity?

Further: is it only the definition of our time as a time of progress that no longer holds up, or does the crisis involve the very usefulness of the notion as a general paradigm of historical thinking, apart from its reference to our present? And in any case what should we call "progress," and what parameters should we use in trying to define its contents?

To get ourselves on the right track, and begin to answer this cascade of questions without having our vision distorted by the circumstances of the moment and their shadows, we must first get used to looking far into the past and becoming familiar with the background of a sufficiently long time scale, which is the only way to a clarifying view.

To this end, I would propose a small mental experiment involving four pictures.

The first requires a dive into our most remote prehistory.[35] Around a million years ago, *Homo erectus* inhabited Africa, Asia, and Europe. Along with *Homo habilis*, who certainly preceded him, he is the first species to which paleontologists, with good reason, assigned the name "man." He had an already complex evolutionary path behind him, going back millions of years, whose outline is clear to us but which still presents obscure and controversial features. Let's imagine for a moment a fragment of his "solitary, poor, nasty, brutish, and short" life. (The words are Hobbes's,[36] and don't refer specifically to lives like the one we're evoking, and certainly don't express current concepts from the anthropological and paleontological point of view, yet they describe fairly accurately the condition we're talking about, which in reality must have been even worse, so harsh it's hard to conceive of.) There is almost nothing in it except eating in order to survive; and possibly to reproduce.

Thanks to the use of their hands, however, those first humans had already developed some abilities that distinguished them dramatically from every other living species—a separation whose origin we still can't explain.

They knew, for example, how to light fires for illumination, cooking, and protection; they used stones, splintered, so they were sharp, and clubs, fashioned from tree branches or animal bones.

So they possessed a small kit of knowledge that they were able to transmit to their kind, and from which derived a certain number of techniques that could be used to manipulate the nature closest to them, to benefit from it. And the erect position—a feat that was by then long-established—allowed them to easily see farther, widening the horizon for actions and choices: and insuring no small advantage in hunting and defense. But, most important, standing, they could observe the night sky continuously, and see stars, whose positions and luminosity were discovered and memorized, and whose arrangement in the darkness suggested images that would modify forever the imagination and inner life of our species. No one, on this planet, had ever done that before.

Let's move forward at a dizzying pace, until we arrive at our present (it's the second phase of the experiment), and think of a place, a hundred meters underground, on the outskirts of Geneva, not far from the tranquil shores of the lake, on the border between France and Switzerland. There is situated the biggest subatomic particle accelerator ever built, the Large Hadron Collider, a gigantic ring, with a circumference of 27 kilometers, which today is being upgraded, to allow even more complex experiments. Through controlled collisions of protons launched at nearly the speed of light, this machine is able to reproduce states of energy and matter close to those which existed at the birth of the universe, at the moment of the so-called Big Bang, many billions of years ago. Such a simulation of the past enables us to comprehend the structure of the fundamental laws of physics that govern our reality.

Let's consider the scientists who designed and built it, and those who use it and interpret its results: men and women who every day work, safely and competently, at the frontiers of our knowledge and the technologies it engenders, and who push them uninterruptedly toward new goals. Let's compare their resources—material and intellectual: devices and concepts, environments and mental states—with those of the distant ancestors evoked before, and measure the distance, but also the continuity that in some way joins them: in both cases we see at work techniques and knowledge, tools and expertise acquired and managed. We may then understand that we are at the two ends of a single, extremely long thread.

Let's then imagine (third phase of our journey) that we have no information about what happened between the two scenarios: the prehistoric and today's. Let's assume that we're in a condition of absolute historical ignorance. We know for certain only that the two pictures refer to the same species (ours); and that between them is a significant lapse of time, but whose extent we cannot assess.

Now let's try (and we've come to the last act) to measure that empty time we've proposed and stock it with possible events, until our (imaginary) gap is filled and a sequence forms that, without relying on any extraneous intervention (an alien presence, say, or a divine illumination), accounts for the passage from the first scene to the second, from the club to the particle accelerator.

So let's ask ourselves: would it be possible to construct a series of events that plausibly connects the two environments described and does not have a comprehensively *progressive* order: that is, does not follow a scheme in which discoveries, inventions, experiments, and reasonings *accumulate* over time, *starting* from the elementary technology of the kindling and controlled management of fire, moving through successive stages and obligatory links (electricity and algebra necessarily before computers, the steam boiler before the nuclear reactor, and iron before steel), and *arriving* at the incomparably more sophisticated technology of the proton collider?

The answer is intuitive, and it is: no. We can invent countless different ways to rewind and project the film of history that leads from the wood fire to the particle accelerator. We can hypothesize routes that are shorter or longer, more direct or more tortuous, more random or more logical with respect to the one that, if with a certain approximation, we know was the only one in effect corresponding to what really happened. But there is one element that we couldn't do without in any of our imaginary reconstructions: on account of which the form of the whole (I repeat: of the whole, not of each segment) necessarily has to arrange itself *according to an irreversible progression*. That is the sense of a "before" and an "after" in time, in which the "after" constitutes a more complex and more advanced moment than those preceding it, and contains them in itself as indispensable premises. In this way it creates a path that represents an advance not only in the strict sense of expertise and technologies deployed but in human intelligence as a whole, and in the grip on reality that human intelligence can exercise from the point of view of comprehension and transformation.

Taking note of this is not without value. It means understanding that the history of the human, at least as regards the cognitive and controlling capacities with respect to the environment that produced that history, and of which it is itself part, has developed in such a way that it can be described only through the paradigm of progress. That means an itinerary that, starting from a degree zero (or very close to zero) of the human's total, unconscious dependence on the natural context he was inserted into, leads him to an immeasurably higher level of mastery, which is, in turn, always capable of further growth.

Thus there is an arrow in the history of our presence on this planet, at least as far as depth of knowledge and mastery of nature is concerned. And it goes in a precise and *progressive* direction that leads from the past to the future, from a lower threshold to one that is infinitely higher.

Our small experiment ends here. But before leaving it, we should note that it offers, with absolute immediacy, another proof, no less important than the one described. And that is that the tendency to acquire increasingly complex technologies that can control with ever greater efficacy the nature that envelops us and lets us exist is profoundly integrated into the specificity of the human, let's say into its uniqueness and its "solitude"[37] as well. It marks human history so pervasively that neither its particularity nor its story would be conceivable or describable without taking account of this fact. The arrow, therefore, not only exists but concerns an essential, morphological aspect of our history, not a minor and marginal side.

The intuition of an irresistible and *progressive* vocation to knowledge and technology has conditioned (but maybe I should say dazzled) a significant segment of twentieth-century philosophy, from Heidegger to Severino (they return), which has been eager to represent its inescapable power as a kind of metaphysical characteristic, endowed with a mysterious, crushing autonomy, and capable of determining from the outside, like an uncontrollable force, our very destiny.

In reality, it's not a question of metaphysics but one of history and anthropology, captured at the genealogical point of their intersection. The mental form of the human is the primary anthropological fact, which, because of an intrinsic structural characteristic, generates a flexible, predatory, and transforming intelligence, ready to modify the external world in the act of knowing it: whether a wood fire or a nuclear fire. That attitude appears as an original element, and with regard to the human we can't go any farther back, even if it's a feature that does not remain unchanged over time—like a motionless pillar—but tends, if somewhat intermittently, to grow and dominate, as it unfolds on the plane of history. It's a cognitive and manipulative capacity that involves the entire natural reality before us, starting with our body, which, in its material physicality, the mind considers—this, too, is a primal trait—an external entity, different from itself. That is to say, an object completely separate from the immateriality of thought and self-consciousness: thus a dialectic is established whose dynamic was fascinating to the most ancient Greek thought.

The relationship between the intelligence of the species and the conformation of nature—between thought and world, if we want to put it like that—is therefore an intrinsically progressive one. That is, it goes from the simplest to the most complicated: from the almost zero of the stick, fire, and the naked eye that looks at the stars at night, to the one hundred (let's say) of the Large Hadron Collider and the radio telescope, which, connected to the computer, listens to the breathing of the universe.

Are these conclusions enough for us to reasonably assume that human history is in its totality *progressive*?

Of course not. Human history doesn't consist solely of its cognitive and transformative side. In other words: our life isn't only the place of technology and the thinking that produces and sustains it.

It's obviously something more, much more. It's made up of social relations that human beings establish in various contexts, bonds that develop between them, and conflicts that set them more or less violently against one another. It's made up of the economic, political, and legal forms that govern societies, and of the power relationships that are established within them, along with their ideological projections. It includes religious, philosophical, artistic experiences; the ideas of morality that guide and justify the behaviors of persons and groups; and so on, for much else besides.

If we take these points of view—or even just one of them—can we say that the same direction can be traced from their perspective, the same arrow oriented in a *progressive* way? At this point the answer becomes more complex, and we have to put it off.

One example is sufficient to understand this. The parabola of the twentieth century, as we've noted, includes the abyss of the Shoah: absolute Evil, the immense power of the negative that gains substance—and what substance!—and becomes history in the form of death: the *mysterium iniquitatis*, or *mysterion tes anomias*, that Paul speaks of enigmatically (II Thessalonians 2:6).

If we consider this event as an exclusive reference point, how can we claim that the century in which it happened represented a step forward on the human trajectory? Shouldn't we conclude from it, instead, that we are looking at not just a frightening regression but a kind of resetting to zero of the relationship between time and civilization—a backward movement of such scope that it forces us to question the very meaning of our species' presence in the space and time of this universe?

We'll return to this problem later. For now let's merely make a note of it. In order to go on using the notion of progress—and we've just seen that we can't do without it if we want to keep trying to understand at least one important part of our past and its relationship to the present—we have to accept that it includes in itself a high degree of fragmentation and discontinuity. That it is, so to speak, a fractured notion, with respect to the multiplicity of planes, levels, and times that structure the complexity of human history. And in any case its truth—the truth of progress—is a relative truth.

Having made this point, we have to move far back in time again, even farther than in the small experiment just described.

When our species appeared, it already had behind it—as noted—a very long evolutionary history that coincides with the history of life on the planet: which continued uninterrupted for more than three billion years, compared with the Earth's age of around four and a half billion.

That duration—which could have been interrupted on several occasions, completely eliminating every biological trace from this corner of the universe—does not contain the linear path of a single necessity, leading from the first organisms directly to us. There is, rather, a tangle of forms, combinations, attempts destined for success or extinction, evolution or disappearance: a feverish and disorderly proliferation, full of irregularities, discontinuities, deviations but also extraordinarily rich. In many, many circumstances, statistical chance was the only thing that set us on the road of a survival and not an extinction. We—as a species—are only a recent, infinitesimal variant of this very intricate plot, even if it's a variant that, in due time, turned out to be capable of achieving a radical, absolutely unpredictable breakthrough: crossing the threshold of self-consciousness and the technological manipulation of natural reality.

For far more than half its existence—for almost three billion years—life remained a prisoner of its most elementary form, limited to reproducing single-cell organisms. It was only around six hundred million years ago that—suddenly, we can say—an authentic explosion of multicellular life took place, the Cambrian era, which saw the birth of all the principal phyla of animals that still inhabit the world: from the insects to the Chordata. It was the first powerful acceleration in the history of the living. From that moment, the chronological scale of events strikingly diminished its distances: from billions of years we move to millions. The measure remains what has been defined as "deep time";[38] that is, a very slow and rarefied flow, a current in which processes unfold in a much colder and more extended way compared with the rhythm that human happenings have accustomed us to, and the sequence of events appears extremely slowed down. And yet from that moment everything begins to move at a livelier pace.

The next stages—as abrupt and unexpected as the first, as far as we know—are marked by massive extinctions ("decimations," it's been said),[39] which might even have involved the majority of life forms present at the time. The first we have a trace of, around forty million years after the Cambrian explosion, is documented by the so-called "Burgess shale."[40] More or less 350 million years later, between the Paleozoic and the Mesozoic, there is a new turning point: when more than ninety percent of marine species disappeared, while the first vertebrates began to move steadily onto land.

Another hundred and sixty million years had to pass before a new catastrophic event. We have reached the late Cretaceous, around sixty-five million years ago. The dinosaurs were part of the new mass extinction, and we have reason to believe that their disappearance significantly encouraged the success of the mammals—who had in the meantime made their appearance—and in particular the most recent arrivals: the primates.

Time now contracts further: no longer hundreds of

millions of years but only tens of millions and then single digits. We've reached the facts that most directly influenced the birth of our species. Between eight and six million years ago the first hominids separated from the group of the big apes. Two or three million years later *Australopithecus afarensis* lived in Ethiopia and, after another couple of million years, *Homo habilis* and *Homo erectus*, whom we've already mentioned.

Then there is a new acceleration, and we are measuring not in millions of years but in hundreds of thousands. Around five hundred thousand years ago another species, probably a descendant of *Homo erectus*, developed in Europe, Africa, and Asia: archaic *Homo sapiens*. And it's possible that from a single one of these populations, a hundred thousand years ago, the Neanderthal *Homo sapiens* [*Homo sapiens neanderthalensis*] was born (though his position in the genealogy of humans is very controversial): he, too, became extinct, or was exterminated (a terrible hypothesis, which bloodies our origins, but not unrealistic).

Anyway, the fact is that for around thirty thousand years only one species has been on the scene, the modern *Homo sapiens*, or *sapiens sapiens*, who used language, reproduced images for pleasure by scratching them on rocks, had ritual memory: a young, aggressive, inquiring, and curious species, emerging after a lengthy labor of selection within a sharply articulated ramification, in which all other paths were dead ends.

Thus it had already been at least a million years (as we've seen) since a different itinerary was superimposed on the evolutionary story of the various species of humans: the itinerary of their early intelligence and the cognitive and manipulative results that it achieved, along with the birth of a culture capable of genuinely developing its own thinking over time.

From here on the rhythms of this new history—now properly cultural, and completely autonomous in relation to the other, which was evolutionary, immensely older and slower—change scale again, and behind the acceleration is a powerful new impetus. Between the rhythms of evolution and those of intelligence—between biological history and cultural history—a divide opens up that is destined to keep getting wider. Compared with the latter, the movement of the former becomes almost invisible. Thus the illusion forms—which persists, even today—of nature as firm and immutable, within and outside us, creating a motionless background for the history of our actions and our thoughts. But this perception, produced by our eye's habituation to speed, is false.

The fact that the most significant acceleration took place only in the most recent stretch of the history of life on our planet, and involved uniquely the tiny fraction linked directly to the development of intelligence, while there are species, even among the primates, that "stopped" many millions of years ago—the detail on account of which everything happens infinitely more rapidly when we approach the human—is the basis of a mental habit that we now have to consider carefully. Because of it we have been led by this velocity to transfer the idea of progress from history that is properly human (from the story of *Homo sapiens sapiens*, I mean) to the total history of the formation of our species—to the history of hominization, that is—extending it to the history of life on Earth and beyond. As if that concept would explain the entire biological history of the planet.

It's an attitude that has a far-reaching consequence, leading us to connect a form's position in the chronology of life to a value judgment of what it represents. Being farther on in time should always imply an improvement, "progress," that is. To be farther back would mean remaining in an unquestionably worse position.

Is it a point of view that we have to accept?

I don't think the belief is wrong in itself, and here I disagree with the great paleontologist Stephen J. Gould,[41] who was also an extraordinarily talented historian. We are facing an essential question in our discussion, which is the legitimacy of expanding the idea of progress to include the history of intelligence (in particular human history) and the history of life—linking them on a single pathway with a very specific direction.

I don't find that opinion incorrect, but on one condition, which to me is crucial. It has to be made explicitly clear that the assessment is carried out exclusively with reference to the emergence, and then the development, of a self-conscious intelligence. That is, the first history (that of life) has to be explicitly subordinated to the second (that of intelligence).

If we maintain that perspective—let's call it humanocentric—it would be difficult to claim that Einstein's brain isn't "better" than that of a tyrannosaurus or even of a gorilla, and that *Homo sapiens sapiens* isn't preferable to the Neanderthal.

But if we don't choose this visual angle, and don't assume self-conscious intelligence and the development of its cognitive capacities as an exclusive reference point; if, that is, we move from a perspective that is intensely centered (on the human) to one that is completely uncentered, from an idea of process that has a subject (and goals) to that of a process without a subject (or goals), everything changes, becoming relative, nuanced, and problematic.

The life of single-cell organisms in the warm oceans of three billion years ago isn't, as such—if we don't compare it to a fixed point of arrival—"better" or "worse" than life in New York or Milan in 2020: it's simply different. It is, literally, another thing. And to speak of progress (or regression) from one to the other would be meaningless. That notion would therefore become completely useless.

Without a center, without a privileged point of view, the "first" is not a "worse" or more backward place but, rather, one that is different, alternative. The story of life would be able to take a variety of pathways, leading to results divergent from those of today: they would be a sign not of "backwardness" but simply of difference. The "Burgess shale" presented a proliferation of varieties never again seen on Earth: maximum diversity, a phenomenon inexplicable by any teleological interpretation (why such a waste of forms destined to a more or less rapid extinction?) but completely plausible given the environment that contained them. Drastically shifting our point of view—and focusing it elsewhere, for example on the triumph of diversity—we could consider that as the most advanced point in the history of life on Earth.

And again. What would have happened to the mammals if the big reptiles hadn't suddenly disappeared? Earth might have remained the planet of the dinosaurs—a boundless Jurassic Park—as it had been for at least a hundred million years before something unpredictable happened, with the result of leaving the way free for the mammals, which until then had been present on the scene in a precarious and secondary way. And finally: where would the Neanderthals be if they hadn't become extinct (or been exterminated) but had prevailed over the first Cro-Magnon men? We can't rule out that they would still be splintering rocks in our place, and in complete solitude.

In this network of discontinuities and ruptures, in this always unpredictable weave of chance and necessity, the most recent human species is—as we've noted—only a tiny element. Our presence is uniquely the result of one of the numerous pathways that life could have taken, many of which might have excluded our existence. An observer who, seventy million years ago, had seen in action a small mammal and an enormous reptile wouldn't have been able to deduce—except in an absolutely hypothetical way—what future was being prepared for the two figures. What comes before in the history of life is potential, richness, virtuality. The after always reflects the selectivity of a choice made; it's the cone of the possible that narrows and closes. If we remain within this single horizon, it makes no sense to speak of progress. In an extraordinarily vast fan of evolutionary lines, all possible in the abstract, chance has chosen ours. There would be nothing more to say.

Another consideration is equally true, however. In this forest of events and possibilities, at every fork, at every extinction, at every success of an evolutionary line, unfailingly, every time, with impressive regularity, a combination compatible with the birth, in its time, of an intelligence able to apprehend and recognize itself has leaped out. This is also valid—on an enormously vaster scale, far beyond the single story of life—in the history of the planet before any biological forms appeared. It can even be extended to the history of the universe as a whole, whose cosmological story developed according to laws favorable to the formation of an environment like ours, able to generate and receive in (relative) safety a life that could produce our species and our intelligence.

There's nothing that allows us—sticking to the realm of scientific investigation—to overinterpret metaphysically the fantastic repetition of circumstances that have consistently favored our arrival. But, historically, we can't hide it. It's a fact, like the others, to take into account.

If we could start the history of life on our planet again from the beginning (to confine ourselves only to that, although we could widen the discussion to include Earth and the universe), we can't be at all sure that it would lead us back to the point where we are. The probability is realistically very high that solutions would emerge different from those which have brought us to our present condition. Perhaps we could have existed for much longer; but it shouldn't surprise us if, in the final scene, in our place a fish was found, a bird, a Neanderthal, or, more simply, nothing at all—which some might even judge the best outcome.

Instead, here we are, however complicated the road behind us has been. And we can't ignore the naked force of that fact. Nor can we forget that the emergence of a part of our history from deep time (the part that concerns our intelligence, not, so far, that which concerns our biological structure and our anatomical design) coincided with the development of cognitive capacities that were able to manipulate reality according to a plan and a technology.

Thus the question is what is the relative position of our species in the history of life, of the Earth, and of the universe. To assess it correctly, I think, we have to try to combine the two different hypotheses I've presented so far. The first (in essence accepted by Gould) I would call the tree and contingency: we are merely a microscopic branch in the great tree of life, the chance product of the occurrence of unique and particular circumstances, and we have no right to distort in our favor the objectivity of this image that marginalizes and reduces us, although it makes us singular and "wonderful."[42] In this picture there is no place for any idea of progress. There is no arrow; and if there is, it doesn't have a precise direction.

The second reading we could call instead the evolutionary primacy of thinking and the transforming attitude. Although we can't in any way deny the complexity and chance nature of the path that preceded us, our very existence, here and now, gives us the right to assess the history of life in this corner of the universe exclusively in relation to its most exceptional, least predictable success: the development of a self-conscious mind.

If we reason like that, we find the arrow and, with it, progress. Everything goes back to moving in a well-defined direction—the one that heads toward us.

Now, to me it seems possible that these two perspectives are not mutually exclusive, as they appear at first glance. We could try instead to hold both at the same time: which is the solution (although more difficult) that I prefer. On the one hand, staying with science, we are in no way authorized to think that our presence as a species signifies the fulfillment of a plan that aimed from the beginning at a determined goal, the birth of a self-conscious intelligence. But, on the other, we can't help considering the advent of the human being as an exceptionally important (and probably rare) result from the evolutionary point of view, nor can we avoid connecting—although on the thread of history alone and not metaphysics—the totality of contingencies that innumerable times have played in our favor on the path that has allowed us to get where we are.

In our past as a species—from its more distant origins, up to the developments that led to the birth of the modern *Homo sapiens*—there is an extraordinary sequence of advantageous circumstances that needs to be evaluated realistically for what it is. This stunning accumulation has to be considered a constituent part of the human story—its most significant tendency, its "momentum trend"—and should become part of our deep culture. And if that leads us to rediscover the arrow, it will be not the fruit of a metaphysical postulate but a result of the importance of our evolutionary history, which has always been headed in the same direction, and that is toward the possibility of our existence. Retrospectively, it reflects only the objectivity of the past and the fact that, yes, we are a species that has so far been very, very lucky. It happens, sometimes (how many times, in the universe?).

In this sense, which I would call "model-dependent

realism conditioned by human self-centeredness,"[43] I think we can also speak of "progress" in the story of life (and a similar argument could be made for the Earth and the universe): from the first single-celled organisms to the mind of Einstein or, if you prefer, of Dante or Mozart.

We can hold on to the two facts we have acquired. The first is that the usefulness of the concept of progress in the history of life depends on the model we employ. The second is that the admissibility of its use in human history should be gauged, in a preliminary way, at least in the short term, in relation to each field we refer to. In both cases, it's clear, we are looking at a legitimate use only under certain conditions, and at a relative truth.

Now let's try to take another step.

Up through most of the twentieth century the two itineraries—the history of life and that of intelligence and civilizations—unfolded along routes that seemed very distinct. The former had as its articulation the "cold" rhythms of the evolutionary story that led to the birth of our species. The other had the much more rapid, "hot" rhythms of human events: events that, in turn, became faster and faster, reaching the vertigo of the present that we're just getting accustomed to.

In fact it should be said that the separation has for a long time been less clear-cut than it appears at first sight (or than we ourselves, for many reasons—religious, ethical, political—want to make it appear). The human, in his incessant work of manipulating reality, very quickly began to modify the nature that surrounds and penetrates him, integrating increasingly larger elements of technological artificiality. (Jacques Monod has written memorably on this.)[44]

A band of "humanized" nature—where nature and artifice are by now nearly indistinguishable—has existed around us for thousands of years, and extends to almost the entire surface of the planet. We long ago began to modify, through cross-breeding and hybridization, the processes of natural selection of many plant and animal species. And not only that: man has also genetically changed himself, his own original natural state—in many instances allowing technologies to operate retrospectively on his biological foundation. (The example of antibiotics is valid for everyone, as they permit even those who don't naturally produce antibiosis to survive, and hence to transmit their genetic inheritance, in that way augmenting the genetic complexity of the species far beyond what nature would have "decided" on its own.)[45]

But despite the increase in these interventions, they have been relatively marginal, and we can say that until now the material conditions of our existence—the basic traits of our genetic structure, our anatomical design, the primary conformation of our attitudes—have been an essentially unchangeable assumption on which the individuality of every life is constructed. They are the natural foundation, given once for all, starting from which our individual existences have developed, as well as that of the species as a whole.

This sort of inviolability—or of violability only at the margins—marked the border between the two different stories. There was the evolutionary story of life in general, and of the species, completely independent of our choices, anchored in the deep and intangible time of the *bios*: the story enclosed and deposited in the structure and physiology of our bodies, in the ontogenetic processes that ceaselessly sum up the phylogenetic path. And there was the entirely and purely human story of our actions and thoughts, always within reach, a reflection of intellects and wills capable of strategies and planning. The latter is completely unbound to the other, but still strictly dependent on it through the subject/object, mind/matter duality that has traversed the entire cultural history of the human—reworked in different forms but always perfectly recognizable in its revival from one context to the other and from one interpretation to the other.

Well, this long separation is about to end, at least in the dimension we've known until now: and the announcement contains a disturbing novelty. After the turning point of self-consciousness, the change we are about to experience, which is already announced by countless signs, is the greatest in the history of humanity.

We have in fact reached a point very close to the frontier that divides the two worlds, the natural and the properly cultural. This boundary will soon be broken down, and the gap between the two stories filled in until—in a future that is more or less close, but already predictable—they come together. And in this reunification is the deeper meaning of the revolution that we are experiencing: with its enormous risks and, at the same time, extraordinary potential.

What has "come naturally" and what is "technologically produced"[46] will become less and less distinguishable, integrated within our own body and, outside, in the ecosystem around us: whose equilibrium will depend less on our purely staying away, on a passive withdrawal, and more on a rational plan of interventions and actively conservationist choices. The natural won't be what is untouched but, rather, what we can and want to defend and make endure as natural. And what will have been until then an unalterable assumption of the human presence in history—the definition of our biological form and its environment—will be the result that we have achieved through our choices.

"*Homo sapiens*, the first truly free species, is about to decommission natural selection, the force that made us. . . . Soon we must look deep within ourselves and decide what we wish to become":[47] that statement sums up the meaning and reach of the turn we are about to take. And so it is. We are moving rapidly toward a history of life oriented by intelligence and not by evolution. *Verum ipsum factum* (what is true is what has been made)—Giambattista Vico's grand formula[48]—can from now on be applied to this last. In other words, we are heading toward a technological takeover of that part of nature more connected to our mind and our existence— our bodies, our habitats, which are about to be transformed into products of our intelligence.

A curtain of silence has fallen over this prediction, though by now it is hardly debatable. In part that's due to the caution of researchers, whose professional habits lead to a sobriety that often borders on reticence, and who fear being taken for some sort of sorcerer's apprentices. In part, it's due also to the superficiality of the media, the intermittent communication between different disciplines—the humanities and the so-called "hard sciences"—and the deficiency and myopia of the public debate on these matters.

But results that to laypeople may at present seem unconnected—genome mapping, genetic recombination, new techniques in fertility, production of stem cells in vitro, preimplantation genetic diagnosis, methodologies of cloning, the initial fusions between bioengineering and nanotechnologies, developments in quantum artificial intelligence—are clearly all heading in a single direction. We're on the point of separating human life completely from the natural state of the species. A sort of extraordinary reverse effect is under way (the conceptualization is Darwin's):[49] the evolutionary drive has ended with the selection of a culture capable of substituting its own technology for the natural selection that produced it. We are facing a change of hands, a solemn changing of the guard, between nature and culture.

I don't think we need be afraid of saying that the present form of the species—our genetic inheritance, which, as we've seen, already includes a degree of inter-action between natural selection and technological inter-ventions—is a fleeting modality. The human changes and changes himself. We've already done it, but now we're about to go through a door that opens onto the unknown: a much more radical and invasive control over the material conditions of our existence, and over the very configuration of our possibilities and talents.

The relationship between mind and body will emerge transformed. The idea of an artificial intelligence that can produce self-consciousness and emotions is the sub-ject of increasingly passionate discussions and diverging predictions. But other scenarios seem more realistic to me, such as those which focus on the possibility of inte-grating both artificial (not biological) intelligence and strictly natural intelligence within the same human-natural system. Our body would be transformed from a purely biological entity into an "integrated" entity, the result of a "bioinformatics" fusion. This is a goal that I think will sooner or later also involve our experience of death, and therefore the relationship between finite and infinite (the finite that dies).

We today are merely transitional figures in the devel-opment of paths like these. We don't know what will be, least of all whether there will ever be *a post-natural fulfillment of the human*: a complete unfolding of his fullness beyond the species; or if the goal will always elude us; or, rather, if it will coincide with the very form of movement, and be subsumed in that.

But one thing we do know for certain: that, however this route is completed, its result will not reproduce what we are now or what we will be at the moment of our definitive parting from natural selection. This is because the human doesn't identify with the species that produced him. From a certain point on, the human will be what we want him to be. We have to know how to prepare for this challenge, and how to accept it, replacing the Frankenstein syndrome, which feeds our fears, with the caterpillar's dream: to one day become a butterfly.

Infinite possibilities open up before us—ranging from the most exciting to the bleakest—before which everything that has already happened is merely a long, tortuous backstory. And we can't help repeating the question we started with: but now it concerns the future and not the past. Can the turning point that is coming into view, and will take the human beyond the confines of the species, be defined as progress? Can the unification of the two different stories—the human and the natural—also be a union in the sense of the idea indicated by that word?

We'll try to sketch out an answer. But first we should ask how far it depends on the result of the imbalance we described earlier between reason and power, between the force of global technological-economic systems and the capacity to control it for the common good, and whether we go toward one of the extremes or, rather, try to find a new balance. And to this, first of all, we must now return.

It should be said right away, meanwhile, that the situation we confront compels us to devise a new paradigm of thought, one that is suited to the reality we are defining, and which therefore holds within a single horizon what up to now was conceptually distinct—natural and human; mind and body; species and the ecosystem that hosts it. Only within this regenerated model of historicity can we test a concept of progress that takes account of the complexity of the path to be interpreted. It's an idea that contains the possibility of setback and retreat, and takes into consideration the existence of discontinuous forms of human development, without, however, losing sight of the long- and very long-term direction of the entire path. And the faster the rhythms accelerate, their tempo increasing to an excited *prestissimo*, the more readily can the flight of the arrow be projected on a scale that reflects the whole of its trajectory.

III
THE FUTURE FOUND AGAIN

We are thus led back to the central point of our story, the imbalance that is sending the world off its axis, and to the speed and intensity of technological progress (now we can use this expression) that have confounded the rest of our culture and our institutions, which are incapable of keeping up with them, as they should.

In fact, to speak of imbalance is not enough. We should, rather, evoke a true fracture, a dangerous gap that splits in two the societies we live in: science and technology flying up one side, dictating the parameters of a new economy; political control, democratic forms, ethical responsibility, interpretative frameworks, planning, and social bonds plodding slowly and uncertainly up another.

More than a decade ago, outlining a situation like this,[50] I seemed to glimpse the possibility of enormous dangers, such as might jeopardize our very survival: the rise of regressive tendencies, blocs of unsustainable privilege, dramatic separations between the generations, irrational choices with disastrous outcomes. I recall that someone even advanced the hypothesis that the twenty-first century might be "our last century."[51]

Thirteen years later, the scenario we have before us is, if possible, even more disturbing. The wedge, far from narrowing, has widened, and the lives of masses of men and women, in the very heart of the West, appear to be enveloped in uncertainty and precariousness, without identities and without reference points, at the mercy of currents they can't control. The great flags of the West—democracy, equality—seem to be wavering and faded, while a previously almost unimaginable disparity in access to the benefits of the technological revolution looms.

In many ways, the imbalance we are experiencing—a social and political form of the world and of the human inadequate to contain and develop the power of the technology that it has produced without getting overwhelmed by it—is the mirror image of a phenomenon that occurred in the very distant past.

I'm alluding to ancient Greece and Rome, where it was technology that stagnated and lagged behind, compared with the dazzling and relatively sudden explosion of other forms of knowledge and other attitudes, such as philosophy, politics, law, ethics, art, and religion, whose creations—the idea of democracy and equality, the grammar of forms of government, the autonomy of law and the regulating force of its formalism, the relation between being and time, the invention of moral law, the elaboration of a monotheism exceptionally powerful in all its versions, literary and visual education to beauty—constituted a legacy that would orient our civilization forever, giving substance to the myth of the "classical."[52]

Thus a correspondence emerges—a kind of symmetrical inversion that, with a long interval, has marked Western history, and which I don't think we've reflected on enough, whereas it should be at the center of our attention.

The ancient societies were poor in technology. The agricultural revolution and the introduction of metalworking were followed by an era of stasis that lasted for almost two millennia, up to the threshold of modernity. The relegation of the practical aspects of production to be considered minor types of knowledge, left to artisans if not to slaves, and fragmented into obscure distinct traditions that lacked meaningful intellectual constructs, was one of the elements at the root of this halt, and of the consequent poverty of machines and energy that long characterized the ancient world.

The standstill went back, in turn, to a more remote fact: to the separation between the impulse to knowledge and transformation of the external environment typical of that world; along with the crushing primacy of the inner "I" and the political bond—the "discovery of the spirit,"[53] as it was called—over the material aspects of existence.

It was this dominance that produced the defining gap: a kind of tilt toward the spirit that was the opposite of the world we live in: a technological void and an extraordinary richness of thinking regarding the human. At the same time, that primacy is what made ancient speculation so powerful—especially the

Greeks', in certain ways the most important—but also reduced it to a prisoner of itself and its metaphysical imagination, without the validation of a genuine investigation of nature.

Nothing was truly worth investigating that did not conclude with self-conscious reflection on the modes and characteristics of one's own activity, or with the contemplation of forms, equilibriums, and principles that were imagined to be buried behind things, secretly and harmonically tuned to the rhythms and power of the mind that was able to discover them.

This set off a sort of radical "dematerialization" of the natural world ("Nature is an end" Aristotle[54] would have said at the height of this tendency: a true flight from physicality, about which it was thought there was nothing more to discover) in search of the first causes that are assumed to be hidden behind the appearances of perceivable reality ("Nature loves to hide").[55]

The tendency was projected onto the metaphysical and spiritual turning point that, with the abandonment of the promising paths opened by Ionic materialism, marked Greek thought from Parmenides and Plato on; from there it was transmitted to all the cultures of the ancient West, defining the ethical and social character—and in some ways even the anthropological structure—of their aristocracies, from the heroic vocation of the Iliad, to the perception of self in lyric poetry and the tragic reworking of myth, up to the development of a rational, abstract discursiveness of thought and a complete practice of politics. In Rome, all of that was expressed in the military attitude, the distributive and organizational talent, and the disciplining knowledge of law, conceived through the paradigm of a formalism as strong as it was effective.

Freedom was identified with mastery of the branches of knowledge tied to social relations in the polis: writing and its canons, music and poetry, rhetorical persuasiveness, self-knowledge ("I have searched myself"),[56] travel and the conquest of new places, training in the use of weapons as an inseparable virtue of the best citizen.

The rest—the practical side of the production of material wealth, the early mechanical and instrumental view of nature that had been formed in archaic Greek and Oriental times—was only the memory of a long-ago subservience to the materiality of the earth and the body, now cut off: something to leave to the slaves, or anyway to the shame of forced labor. It took an epochal leap and the end of an entire civilization to resolve the split.

But there is much more in this sort of counterpoint between ancient and modern that we are trying to unearth. It concerns the core of our argument, and goes back again to the long-term effects of technology and its unfolding.

From time to time, in both ancient and modern societies, the technological level achieved, affecting the general social form of the contexts in which it appeared, was also in the end crucially important to aspects of culture that at first sight might seem less conditioned by its development.

A single example will suffice: what led the ancients—almost without exception, despite the profundity, also ethical, of their reflections—to consider slavery and the inferiority of women to be fundamental elements of any civilization worthy of the name, portraying them as natural features that couldn't in any way be modified? (There are passages in Aristotle that today sound literally chilling, in this sense).[57] It would be difficult to offer an explanation of what to us seems a catastrophic failing, if we based it only on a conceptual weakness, on a theoretical breakdown. From that point of view, Aristotle certainly isn't less valuable than, let's say, Rawls: and yet an abyss divides their reflections on these subjects, despite the American scholar's obvious debt to the Greek philosopher.

The point is that it would be impossible to explain the difference purely in terms of the history of philosophical thought, without also taking into account the technological contexts (with their economic and social consequences) in which answers with such different substance are formulated. An extremely rigid hierarchy of roles and functions—an ironclad division of labor—was indispensable, in the conditions of production in ancient societies, in order to sustain the weight of organizations complex enough to insure at least to small minorities the time and resources necessary for the development of a superior culture: to allow Aristotle to think. And without the subjugation of one part of humanity by another, in the form of slavery and the subordination of women, the social result needed for the type of civilized coexistence we just described[58] would never have been achieved with such speed and orderliness.

And correspondingly, shifting in time, how to explain the peculiarly modern idea of the emancipation of all humanity—without any distinction of gender, ethnicity, class—except by linking it to the fact that we have reached a technological threshold allowing the existence of much more fluid, flexible societies, no longer in need of hierarchies and roles fixed by coercion and dependence: a goal unthinkable in the ancient world.

In other words: how to account for the difference, except by connecting the achievement of modern results to the history of capitalist organization and labor, not to mention the industrial and technological revolution that made them possible?

Of course, all that doesn't mean imagining that we can deduce in a linear way the history of thought and ethics from the history of the technology that went along with them. And no one would maintain that the only difference between the Athenian philosopher and the one from Harvard—to return to them—is the fact that one knew electricity, the steam engine, and General Motors, and the other didn't; and that the former couldn't conceive of the work of his looms (as he himself says in a page made fascinating by and anticipating subsequent history),[59] except as the labor of slaves. All it means is knowing that without steam looms, electricity, and turbine engines, and without the great factory systems of the modern West, it would be very difficult to imagine thought like Rawls's; and that, on the other hand, we can't even remotely imagine what Aristotle would have written, faced with the same reality.

We can thus take another step. Thought about the human and thought about the history of technology do not proceed according to the same rhythm, as we've said. Between the two paths wide gaps can open up, and in fact have opened up: what remains of ancient science is only archeology, but the presence of Sophocles, Plato, Aristotle, and the Roman jurists is still a constituent of our modernity.

And yet the journeys—however distinct and dissimilar—are not independent. A narrow but crucial tie binds them, in the sense that technology—whatever level it reaches—defines the limits of the range of possibilities within which the thought about the human that goes along with it moves. It determines, so to speak, the confines.

As technology acquires power, its transformative force becomes greater, its capacity for intervention in the reality both inside and outside us is more incisive, and thought about the human is all the more able to broaden its field of vision. It gains the strength to generate new connections, and to proceed unfettered by ties and cultural and social constrictions that were merely the reflection of its preceding condition of inferiority, of its lack of command over external reality, both natural and social.

Said differently and more succinctly: the power of technology is liberating. Or rather: it creates the conditions that enable thought to be free and to conceive the human in his wholeness and in the infinite potential contained in his finiteness.

Let's pause again, and for the last time, on the history of ancient and modern slavery, to fully understand the meaning of what was just said.

We have observed that in ancient times slavery was considered a condition that couldn't be eliminated; and this stated necessity was long held to be the manifestation of a natural law. Nor did Christianity really avoid this tendency. So called ancient humanism, from the Stoics of the Hellenistic age to Terence, to Seneca, to the philanthropic emperors of the second century so loved by Gibbon, and the bishops of the post-Constantine church, never went beyond the generic principle according to which it would be reprehensible to be cruel to one's slaves for no reason.[60]

The idea that slavery was an aberrant institution struggled to advance in the modern age. And it was only when, on the wave of the industrial revolution, capitalist organization took a decisive upper hand even in the former colonial countries, offering an economically successful alternative to the use of slave labor—an alternative that no ancient politician or jurist or master of ethics could ever observe—that what by us today is universally judged a contemptible practice ended with its complete disappearance.

It's evident that in this case the technological leap wasn't transformed as such into an ethical judgment. That conclusion would mean surrendering to a completely unjustified determinism. Technological advance was limited only to creating the conditions—previously nonexistent—that made possible a drastic change in the makeup of the forms of conscience and moral paradigms. How this change came about, and how it developed, belongs not to the history of technology but to that of humanistic culture, of ethics and society.

We can now return to the idea of progress.

We have already seen that the history of technology, an important aspect of human history, has adhered completely to that paradigm. And the statement is true in at least two ways.

First of all, because that history proceeds by means of successive and connected accumulations, even though it follows unpredictable rhythms, with long intervals and sudden accelerations compared with the timing of other itineraries. And then because if we take as a point of reference the capacity for knowledge and for control over the conditions of the human—which is a fact, although always relative, completely within the establishment of technology as such—we see that its development leads from a beginning near zero to an end point not yet achieved but already visible, where this control becomes total. We have spoken therefore of an intrinsically progressive relationship between thought and world.

Yet we have also observed that this progressiveness can't extend mechanically and uniformly to all of human history. We have to see it as a relative and fragmented notion, which can allow scientific and technological accelerations and advances to coexist with moments of even catastrophic crisis in other fields and spheres: deviations that have been typical of modernity in particular, from the start, and which have become stronger and riskier in the course of the twentieth century and the first decades of the twenty-first.

In the short term, these misalignments have produced serious consequences, including uses of technology turned directly against humanity, seriously compromising the integrity and variety of its wealth: from the use of firearms in the annihilation of pre-Columbian America—mobility and destructive capacity, sails and cannons—to the chemistry of gases in the trenches of Ypres and the Isonzo, and the scientific planning of mass death in Auschwitz and Dachau, or the politics of the Shoah.

But it is equally true that, if we expand the scale of reference and consider longer time periods—entire blocks of history and not only single episodes or narrow segments—modernity has always managed, sooner or later, at least so far, to develop the strategies necessary to make up for the deviations, to control in a not too destructive way the new technologies, and stop the more dangerous disruptive surges, so as to emerge from their inferno.

Nuclear weapons have been used in war once in almost a century. It was an atrocious event, but one that remained isolated. And other cases regarding the failures and lacerations that we feel, belatedly, as indelible stains and unthinkable mistakes have been condemned and reviled, even if after the fact, and those judgments, including the most radical, are now commonly accepted.

The slave trade between Africa and America that for centuries employed the ships and merchant companies of the greatest European sea powers appears repugnant to us today. And horror not only at the unspeakableness of the Shoah but also at that petty, creeping anti-Semitism that was tolerated by and poisoned so much of popular and bourgeois European society in the nineteenth and twentieth centuries, acting as a culture medium for the explosion of Nazi ferocity, is now an integral part of our most well established and common public discourse.

Thus our final thesis has to be formulated in these terms. Technological progress dramatically increases the power of the species, and that acquisition creates in the abstract the possibility of greater freedom for all humanity. But the disappearance of long-endured chains and the emergence of new transformative capabilities do not always and immediately lead in a single direction; rather, they open up to numerous solutions, all the more varied the greater the freedom gained, and including the worst, even if we have so far avoided the most catastrophic:

Nazism didn't win and there hasn't been a global nuclear war.

In other words, technology and power open up spaces that can be filled in very different, even extreme ways, taking paths that may be distant from one another: leading to the annihilation of the human or, on the contrary, to his complete fulfillment. Freedom and power mean this, as well: the multiplication of options, ranging, in specific historical situations, from a total negative to totally positive.

But the choice between the different paths isn't random; and this point is crucial. It depends on the relation established between the level of technical progress reached in a particular era and the widespread capacity—social, political, institutional, moral—to manage the consequent power, orienting it to come as close as possible to an ideal condition where it can be used to protect the integrity of the human, in its granular singularity, and to homogeneously increase its levels of self-consciousness and autonomy.

The relationship between power and control didn't amount to much in antiquity, because of the technological poverty of the era: when, that is, there was little to choose from, and submission to natural constraints was overpowering and didn't leave many alternatives. And this is why although the ancients appear in many ways close and similar to us, they suddenly reveal the abyss that puts them at a distance; and although their thinking appears to be a foundation of our civilization, it also reveals dizzying failures and voids.

But that relationship has reached extraordinarily high and complex levels in the modern world, where—because our mind is far less subjugated to the environment that surrounds us, and its capacity to transform it is much greater—the possible choices have increased exponentially: to welcome evil, but also finally to think of the human in its entirety and in its unlimited multiformity.

The calibration of that relationship therefore defines the degree of responsibility that objectively we have to meet. The greater the force of domination and power, the greater the dangers that this force entails. At the same time, however, the ability to perceive the integrity of the human as an absolute value is strengthened, and this clarity of perception is much more evident for the moderns than it was for the ancient Greeks or Romans. The vision, which becomes sharper as technology advances, is centered precisely in the recognition that all that is human, even in its infinite diversity, is equal—the perception of its integrity as full awareness of its equality. This awareness is not of parity between individuals, who exist as diverse, but, rather, of a more profound uniformity, extra-individual and yet fully historical and concrete—"the human" that runs through all individuals, giving them form and substance, and that needs to be recognized, protected, and valued as such.

There are, in turn, two consequences of this type of

equation between transforming power and its rational control.

The first is the more important for the purposes of our story. It leads to a discovery that appears counterintuitive with respect to the perception we have of our present condition, and might even seem contradictory to what we've said so far, but it is, rather, only a resulting development. And that is, it pushes us to trail the existence of a direction—of an arrow again—also in the events and processes in human history that are not immediately traceable to technological progress: to find, at least as a trend and over the long term, the thread of an internal progression. This would be a non metaphysical track entirely resolved within the sequences of events that contain it, and so never uniform and linear, and always exposed to the risk of breaking or of offering unforeseen twists and new knots. But still it's a thread, tenacious enough to have endured up to now.

And in fact if we assume as a point of reference the values achieved by the equation we've delineated—and as always we're talking about a relative point of view—we realize that the path of history runs in a single direction. This is signaled by the tendency for increasingly broad swaths of humanity, compared with its totality, to reach the highest possible ratio between the available technological power—and therefore control over one's own conditions of existence—and recognition and validation of one's own existence. It's a goal that history has so far kept shifting farther off, even though the movement has been intermittent: defining a movable frontier beyond which the responsibility of the human increases not only regarding himself but toward life as a whole and the nature that is around it.

This push forward evidently transcends the development of technology as such, and constitutes an original characteristic of the general history of the species: the plot that gathers it whole, without residues, and projects it toward the future.

The second consequence of the power-control equation makes it clear that technological progress, with the orientation of the arrow, is an indispensable premise for the other arrow—the arrow of the rest of history, so to speak—to have substance and movement. In other words, for the process of human self-recognition to get started. Leaving aside the metaphor: without technological progress, human progress as a whole would be inconceivable.

At this point the conclusion is unavoidable.

Technological progress defines the general shape of the *entire* history of the human, in the infinite variety of its particular aspects. That doesn't mean that the push forward assured by this advance is mechanically transferred from one level to the next, and that everything proceeds together at the same time. It means that all of history reflects and reworks in each of its parts the progress of technology, and constitutes so to speak an interpretation of it, which can lead in different directions: toward the abyss or toward an increasingly complete fulfillment of the human. The choice depends on the relationship achieved each time between control and power, between reason and domination. And it's a relationship that, in the long term, has so far tended to come down on the side of reason.

Thus history as a whole has a direction, and moves like an arrow, even though it often doesn't appear that way to us, who are misled by the false appearances of a journey that only in the long term reveals its genuine trajectory.

And it's also for this reason—that it has a direction (or at least has had up to now)—that ours is a singular and precious history. Not because it has a transcendent value (that is a problem that I deliberately avoid) but, rather, because it's unique, the result of a distinctive evolutionary and cultural path, which, starting from the origin of the universe, and then of life in the oceans of this planet, arrived at each of us: me, at home, writing, and you who are now reading.

The twentieth century and the turbulent start of the twenty-first, with the burden of their fractures, have obscured the perception of this path: of its meaning and of the place occupied by our difficult present. This is one of the products—certainly among the most dangerous—of the twentieth century, in which the unprecedented manifestation of Evil acted as a witness and prologue to an increase in human power such as history had never before known. *Roma quanta fuit ipsa ruina docet*:[61]

the very dimensions of the catastrophe reveal the power that made it possible, and the infinitely greater power that was about to enter the scene. This is the horror—which Klee's angel didn't even want to see—that becomes the herald of a new era. But not even the most terrible tragedy could change the direction of the arrow.

Within a few decades the technological leap of the late twentieth century had modified all the scenarios of our civilization. A world that had taken two centuries to absorb the social traumas of industrialization found itself hurled in a completely unforeseen direction. It had to struggle with an immensely more gripping revolution, and was forced to reckon with a dislocation of economic power—a literally regenerated form of capital—that not only made trouble everywhere for the tools of politics (and of democracy), developed to function in a very different context, but provoked sudden vortexes of inequality and exclusion that no one knows how to deal with.

In the wave of change and the conflicts it produced, the progressive meaning of the connection between technology and liberation was disastrously obscured, at least in the West, under the weight of social and cultural rubble—the collapse of entire classes and their institutional and intellectual scaffolding—which seems to fill (and in part has truly done so) our entire field of vision. The golden age of modern labor—a universe constructed around the industrial production of material goods—ended in the space of a few years, and the epilogue provoked a mainly cultural shock from which we can't recover.

The first task of our intelligence today is to find a way out of the trouble. But we have to be clear right away that we won't emerge by trying to suppress the power of technology. Even if it were ever possible—and I don't think it could be, for the reasons I've tried to make clear in these pages—it's too late now. The impulse is unstoppable: and on it depends—and will increasingly depend—the entire economy of the planet.

The only practicable way is to adjust our civilization, so that we are capable of sustaining the impact of the change and guiding it; of recalibrating yet again, and at its highest point, the relationship between control and power, between technology and liberation. And it's in this sense that—it seems to me—the pressure of that new, youthful sensibility whose first tremors are traversing the planet should be understood: a culture that is born global because it knows no other way of existing except through the global; and whose ecological anxiety betrays a need for alternatives and for a new construct of the human, which at the moment represents the greatest resource we have to work with.

To succeed, to rediscover the arrow, we have to first of all renew contact with our future, and imagine this step as if it were the real reconquest of a lost territory that still belongs to us, and without which we can't live.

For this undertaking we need two weapons, which have been missing in these difficult years. In the first place, thought—I mean new thinking about the human, and not only about technology and scientific knowledge, to rectify our imbalance, and bring back into equilibrium the values of the equation we've been talking about. Second, a new politics: that is to say, a new form of democracy, because politics coincides with democracy, otherwise it's not politics but a grotesque replacement. And these two weapons should be used together, since either they are able to mutually sustain and complement each other or both miss their target. Only their combined use—thought and democratic politics—can allow technology to express its liberating function toward the human, to confirm, that is, the direction of our history.

Thinking (about the human) without a political horizon to refer to becomes an intellectual exercise that can never be measured against the effectiveness of the real. Hegel understood this well, as did Marx. And Spinoza before them had intuited it. And even Heidegger and Gentile—if in a way that led them over the edge of the abyss—were aware of it: so to speak, all great modern metaphysics.[62]

But politics (democracy), in its turn, without new thinking becomes what unfortunately we have today right before our eyes in most of the West: a sterile game of power confined to the present alone, which—in the extended illusion of an eternal here and now—has at stake an increasingly minor share of control, to the point of complete irrelevance. Politics isn't an eternal form; it, too, is a product of history, like democracy, after all. It had a birth, and we could see it die without knowing what to replace it with, except nightmare scenarios.

I'm not going to discuss this risk in what follows: the subject would lead us too far from our intentions, which concern only the conceptual and cultural outlines of the question we're addressing, and it would be more valuable to conclude our reflections on these.

The reconquest of the future needs to bring back into play the idea of progress and the connection between technological development and human liberation: the genuine heart of our story. Only the prospect of this relationship can allow us to hold on to a positive vision of the time that awaits us, capable of reconnecting us to the lost thread that has sustained our journey.

That has to mean casting the foundations of a new theory of the human—the basis for a cultural, political, and moral anthropology that has integrated technology into itself—that can accompany and orient the revolution we are experiencing (which has barely begun), just as a new anthropology and a new theory of the human were set forth by European thought from Hobbes to Hegel, if with many variants, differences, and even internal contradictions. This was an intellectual season that accompanied and oriented the great epoch of early industrial and capitalist modernity: exactly the world we've lost.[63]

At the center of that construct the paradigm of the "individual" stands unopposed, tied by countless threads to the Christian concept (in the Lutheran and Calvinist version adopted by Hegel) of the "person." The primacy of the bourgeois Christian individual-person—the sovereignty of the personal, as it has been called[64]—is from then on so overpowering in our tradition that it is now identified with the very form of the human, as if it were the neutral reflection of a natural fact, and not a social and cultural construct, however extraordinarily potent: and therefore always a historical product, to be considered as such. And even the line of thought that sought to oppose to it the model of the collective—with the "we" in place of the "I"; the line that goes from Rousseau to Marx and arrives directly at the successive socialist doctrines—in the end assumed as inalterable its basic features, to the point of the paradox, outlined by François Furet,[65] that we are incapable of considering the social except by starting from the individual.

The moment has come to say plainly that this figure, however glorious and charged with the past, no longer—or at least not by itself—coincides with the entirety of the human, or express all its wealth and potentialities, as they are emerging from the transformation taking place around us.

I believe in fact that in certain circumstances it can even become a regressive form, which behaves like a brake in regard to the developments we're already starting to see. And though I wouldn't go so far as the radical ideas of Miguel Benasayag, who sees in the individual, in particular in his contemporary consumer and hyper-acquisitive version, the true enemy of the planet,[66] it seems to me that the self-consciousness of a species about to breach the biological margins imposed by its evolutionary history needs to get past the individual as the exclusive paradigm of its representation.

This doesn't mean that the person-individual form, developed so successfully by modernity, should be considered outmoded, and that we can now do without it. It means only that it's time to free the human form from the monopoly—and what a demanding monopoly!—of that mechanism and its cultural projection (ethical, political, legal), in order to integrate it with other constructs (I'll say something about that in a moment) in a complementary relationship between different forms that can coexist with, rather than mutually exclude, one another. This could become one of the next goals of our history.

And it's exactly what I mean now when I maintain—as I have for a long time[67]—that we urgently need a new humanism: a philosophy that gives us an image and an ethics of the human that are able to go beyond the individual. Its realization—or at least its start—is, it seems to me, one of the overriding conditions that would enable us to again think of the future in terms of progress and liberation (it's the same thing, as we've seen) and bring back trust in ourselves, securely, beyond the bitterness of the moment.

We have to look, I think, at an objective expansion of the human, in the entirety of his complexity and his differences, as if at a unique, total subjectivity—the global subjectivity of the species, which doesn't say "I" but speaks only in the third person. Thus it would use the language of the impersonal, which is able to express an infinite value, that of the self-conscious life, unique (as far as we know today) in the infinitude of the universe. This is the only way—probably—to separate the idea of equality from the historical-anthropological form of the individual, with which it has problematically lived for all of modernity, and rejoin it, without contradictions at last, to its truer and more fitting dimension: that of complete impersonality. This last is an element reflected in turn in every biologically autonomous fragment of the human—in every individual, to take up the lexicon of our tradition—which always has to be considered, historically and politically, the particle of a whole, primary and indivisible.[68]

In order to regain equilibrium, the global economy—which is more than ever a mode of the capitalist organization of the world, and therefore itself a historical form destined sooner or later to extinction—needs to be confronted by an equally global subjectivity, and that can't be established except by the impersonality of the human as a whole. This impersonality becomes the subject (the oxymoron is only apparent), but to become the subject without negating itself it has to construct its subjectivity entirely by inclusion, as a comprehensive form.

The critical importance of this step is evident if we consider a crucial question that we're going to have to face soon, and that will require sharing a new border: the availability and concrete use of technologies that, through increasingly sophisticated gene-editing processes, will allow us to modify the biological condition of the species so profoundly that the very structure of the relationship between "body" and "person" will change.

But if the "person" can become the subject-object of a process of transformation of its conditions of existence, how not to see that only by getting outside it can we find a standard to serve as a norm to regulate such a possibility? And where to find that possibility, if not in the global subjectivity of the human, taken as a guide and as an ethical and legal value, far beyond the dialectic between the individual-person and the state-person that has up to now depleted modernity?

It seems to me that, when we picture situations like the one just described, the first general principle of conduct should be the rule according to which the genetic equality that we have inherited from the evolutionary history of the species we are going beyond is an inviolable asset; and so every proposal for an inheritable modification of our biological patrimony should be considered only if it is available, in conditions of absolute parity, to all humanity. That is, complete genetic uniformity should be preserved intact at the moment of the handoff from nature to technology, and should be considered an absolute value, transmitted to us from our evolutionary past and projected beyond the species itself. In that post-natural figure of the human that we should inaugurate under the sign of equality is our finest and most precious attainment, both evolutionary and cultural (thanks to technology): a goal that we must never take for granted as achieved but always consider an objective to protect.[69]

The history of technology and the history of human self-determination are not the same thing (as we've said) and do not proceed together. But the first is what gives the second the possibility of existing. And if in the latter we can trace an arrow—and we have seen that we can, in the long term—we owe this to the direction of the other. We are looking at two arrows cocked at the same time by twin bows that aim, separately and from different angles, at the same target. Their course participates in the coming into being of being in the structure of the universe, which we are able to perceive in the form of history, and only history; human intelligence is part of this history, even if we cannot know of what dimensions, occupying what position, and with what fate, at least for now. And this uncertainty, more than anything else, fills with apprehension the thoughts that reflect on it: *inquietum est cor nostrum.*[70]

Awareness of the past—including the past that precedes the species—helps us concentrate on the challenge that awaits us: a trial that requires us to adjust the capacity for social, ethical, political, and legal construction to a dizzying technological leap (just begun and already overwhelming), in such a way as to sustain its effects and orient them in the direction that has so far been maintained, despite terrible breakdowns and dark twists: the direction of greater freedom for the human, and a greater capacity to understand and fulfill himself. In this sense, we can say, I think, that the step we have before us, which will lead the human—a human who has seen Evil become history—beyond the natural confines of the species, will be a time of progress: probably the most important on our path.

Thus Klee and Benjamin's angel was wrong: there was something that resisted and endured, beyond the horror and beyond the ruins, on account of which it was worthwhile to look.

The historian's profession, if he makes good history, can be a job full of hope.

Virus and Ideas
A Sort of Afterword

This book has had—by chance—a rare privilege. The ideas it presents have been subjected to the harshest, most unimaginable test, a test that sheds on them an unexpected, inescapable, stark light of truth.

And how have those ideas held up to the impact with the dramatic facts? How does an essay that tries to reformulate the concept of progress manage to sustain the encounter with such a catastrophic episode, a global epidemic that has overwhelmed the planet?

Obviously it's not for the author to give an answer, or at least the last word is not his. In this case, however, made exceptional by circumstances, I want to offer not a judgment but, rather, a kind of testimony to the work done, and of the relationship I'd like it to have with the times we're going through.

I consider the epidemic a sign from history: strong, alarming, violent. If we know how to read it for the best, if we can get from it all its "prophetic" meanings and act accordingly, it won't have come in vain. Otherwise, it might be only the forerunner of a still more serious, perhaps irremediable devastation.

As I anticipated at the start, I believe that what is happening confirms the points developed in the book. It's as if a kind of historical experiment—by virtue of an unexpected event—had been carried out, in which the accounts are balanced in the end, and the circle of proof closes ever more tightly.

Rapidly, for the convenience of the reader, I will try to indicate the lines of this convergence between facts and ideas.

Science and technology. The first evidence to emerge from the past months is confirmation of the greater weight that technology and science have now assumed in determining the course of our lives—a theme of this book.

The history of mankind is marked by epidemics, and they have left significant traces in our memory, from the Athenian plague described by Thucydides to those which, along with cholera, periodically ravaged Europe between the Middle Ages and early modernity (Boccaccio, Manzoni), and to the Spanish flu and polio outbreaks in the last century, before the Salk and Sabin vaccines.

The processes that start them are all part of the biological context into which our species is inserted. But if their mechanisms can always be traced to this long-term natural background, the social form that epidemics assume—how they spread, how much and how rapidly they circulate, how they're distributed, how they're treated, what death rate they develop, how they are absorbed by our culture—varies case by case, and depends on history alone.

In that sense, Covid-19 is the first epidemic in the world that from the start (or almost) has been subjected to a total, global medicalization, and has been accompanied by a wave of information (even if with some major mistakes) that has never stopped. Nothing similar had happened before. An abyss separates it, in this regard, from the so-called Spanish flu of a century ago, which was experienced almost in silence, despite the frightening number of victims (tens of millions). Now, on the contrary, the uninterrupted flow of news regarding the illness—along with the global, contemporaneous character of the contagion, and the dimensions of the health response, to the point of mass vaccination—is the real novelty of the event, much more than its strictly clinical aspects.

In this circumstance, science and technology appeared clearly for what in fact they are: the guardians of humankind, guarantors of its existence. Their protocols, their procedures, their prescriptions have become for the first time the measure of a universally accepted globality, no longer confined, as it had been until now, to the single dimension of the market and goods but able to affect life itself, and put it on the line.

Anyone who still had doubts about the *progressive* function of such knowledge and practices, of their capacity to project beyond the capitalist shell that still contains them—this is a crucial point that I can't dwell on here, but that should be developed at length—has been resoundingly refuted. Technology and science are not a power alien to us, which determines us from the outside. They are our daughters: they're us. They are our reason at work: the crucial product of our history. This mass reappropriation of science on the part of its people—a kind of reconciliation and recognition never before experienced so intensely—has been an unusually powerful phenomenon, which leads to hope.

Our place in nature. According to an opinion that has had a substantial following in these months—and of which several versions have been heard, some more cultivated than others—the epidemic is in some way the effect of a nature that has been recklessly violated, or excessively strained and harassed. It has been defaced by an accelerated urbanization that has led to "a jungle in the cities"; by the disappearance of age-old agrarian landscapes, replaced by human beehives where millions of people are concentrated, packed one on top of another; by eating habits that mix ancient peasant cultures and new attitudes of mass consumption. The illness should remind us, however, that we are part of a natural habitat to be respected and not overwhelmed; and that we are not absolute masters but only a small negligible fragment of it.

I don't deny—obviously—that there are important elements of truth in this view, which shouldn't be underestimated. The capitalist economy—this, not technology as such—possesses intrinsic reckless and predatory features, which, if not carefully controlled, tend to multiply inequities and social and environmental wounds whose extent is unpredictable.

What absolutely should not be accepted, it seems to me, is the thinking often concealed behind these justified reminders, the idea that our problems result simply from the fact that we have gone *too far* in subjecting nature to technology: that we have crossed an insuperable limit, and that the only way to save ourselves is *to turn back*, while we still have time.

All our history demonstrates that this is not so: and this small book has tried to remind us of that.

Before this supposed limit had been crossed, and nature was intact in its presumed sacredness, people died like flies. Epidemics and food crises (the famines that history books are full of) provoked genuine periodic decimations in European populations (and no retrospective summary counts can be kept of the massacres on other continents). These deaths were accepted by common opinion as inevitable "natural" events, when not as merited divine punishments. And reaching the age of sixty was a challenge that few met.

All this has been forgotten, luckily, at least in the West, and will soon be forgotten in the rest of the world. Violated nature can feed billions of people, and could do it even better if there weren't atrocious distortions due not to the arrogance of technology but to that of politics or economics. When, on the other hand, the earth was still uncontaminated, it barely supported no more than some hundreds of millions of inhabitants.

The crucial difference between this crisis and those past lies in the fact that today we give the greatest importance to life—to the single life, in its granular individuality, almost everywhere in the world. It's a change that has allowed mankind an incomparable jump in quality. And thus a number of victims that a century ago would have passed almost unobserved raises alarms and horror. At least until the beginning of the twentieth century daily existence in the European countryside was frighteningly harsh, even without epidemics. And when these were unleashed—without doctors, without hospitals, without disinfection, *without technology*—the unimaginable happened.

The point is that today we have hugely raised the threshold of our defenses and our attention to the human—to every life, wherever it is—and this is reflected in the way we face emergencies. We finally have a very high guard, even if it's never high enough. And only the *progress* of technology has made possible such a critical ethical and political leap, which should be evident at the end of this book, and which has been seen clearly in these months, when our moral sensibility impelled us first of all to ask for more science, and more technology.

The answer to the problems of the present is therefore ahead of us, not behind. We have to continue on the path, not retrace our steps. It's true, the human is *still* tied to the naturalness of the species. And that means that there is still a network of links and compatibilities to consider, which was probably not done in the current situation. But our entire history has been heading in the direction of diminishing the strength of these bonds, certainly not increasing it. As long as they endure, we have to anticipate the consequences and act with common sense and attention, knowing, however, that sooner or later in our future we will break that knot, not celebrate its omnipotence. That is, we'll gain complete control of the nature around us, which also includes its conservation; we won't perpetuate our submission, which every day becomes less.

Achievement of the goal—the emergence of the human from the natural form of the species, as this book has said—requires a journey that is full of risks. And that happens as the power we're able to deploy becomes greater but not yet great enough to achieve a complete liberation; while the dangers of not controlling it for the best become just as great, creating situations of serious inequity. And it's in this gap, which the book points out, that even very grave incidents take place, like the one we're now caught up in, and that could repeat, in even worse forms, if we're not cautious and vigilant. Many things will have to change.

Yet we mustn't confuse criticism—even the most intransigent—of our inadequacies and mistakes with rejection of the technological gains that have made it possible and carried us so far. It would be like repeating the mistake of the English factory workers who, in the early nineteenth century, destroyed the new machines, believing them directly responsible for the ruthless, crushing exploitation of labor. They mistook what technology made possible but not inevitable for what economic power and politics made historically invincible. We are more *advanced* than they were, and see more clearly and farther.

Global governability. This book talks about the gap between power and control as one of the great dangers that our world is exposed to. I think the current health crisis is a direct consequence of the imbalance I was trying to point out before.

The technological revolution has unified the world economy, and has made very different social universes similar, if not actually uniform, integrating consumption, needs, expectations, behaviors. But it hasn't created a global system of governance for the unprecedented "social fusion"—the needle's eye of our future—made up of exchanges, contacts, mutual contaminations, transplants, overlaps, hybridizations. Let me be clear: I'm not talking about politics—it's still too soon for that. I'm still referring to sociality: work, education, health, culture, and much else. These are enormous human spaces, in which only the presence and movement of goods and finances seem to be regulated.

It's in this void that the epidemic originated and

developed. The power of technology caused it to spread rapidly and widely, multiplying instantly and on a global scale the opportunities for contagion. But that very power did not protect us, as it could have—at least in the initial phase, containing and anticipating the spread of the virus—because it wasn't translated into global governance of health, that is, universally accepted and practiced mechanisms of transparency and prescription, like those of the capitalist economy and the technologies that enable it.

And this lack of alignment between social rationality and technological power—power that makes innovation possible but does not protect us from its risks—is a clear example of the imbalance the book discusses. Because of the way the argument was formulated, it might perhaps have seemed too abstract, and yet history was immediately charged with making it more concrete, demonstrating with a tremendous example.

Still, the crisis—once it exploded—also revealed something else: that the world not only is ready to welcome the governance that's been lacking but demands it, at least as regards the most exposed sector, health. And I will go farther. In some measure it has even constructed it: for now in bits and pieces, spontaneously and from the bottom, so to speak (and this method of proceeding in fragments may be a sign for the future). We have seen this in the tenacious, unprecedented collaboration between scientists of all nations; in the common, not simple identification of shared protocols (despite the delays caused by politics, which is always slow: it's the curse of our time); in the universal adoption of the same behaviors, with cities deserted from Paris to Wuhan, from New York to Auckland—an unprecedented sight, which spoke to us not only about the contagion. It also told us about the invincible communitarian and supportive aspect of the human, which the objectivity of science and technology has finally agreed to let emerge in all its force.

Let's not waste this lesson. It's a result to start from, without waiting for the next wave.

A note. The abuse in Italy, and throughout Europe, of the metaphor of war to describe our situation (front line, front, trenches, behind the lines, enemy, battle, weapons, the fallen . . . and so on) has been among the most misleading and harmful cultural phenomena of these months. Within certain limits, it's true, recourse to the old (the war) to explain the new (the medical difficulties of the epidemic) is inevitable. But, once a certain threshold is crossed, insisting on the analogy only exacerbates misunderstanding, makes us mentally lazy, and keeps us from comprehending the reality that has to be confronted.

And then let's say it, once and for all. This isn't a war. It's a serious and dangerous emergency. It's not an enemy. There is an insidious mistake to correct, occurring not on a battlefield but in one of those points of intersection between the natural and the human-cultural

which are still crucial for our civilization and, if neg-
lected, can put our very existence at risk. There's enough
to frighten us. But we're not at war. Fears change: they,
too, are only history.

NOTES

I. THE ANGEL'S GAZE

This short essay is based on two previous books of mine, which I will refer to frequently: *Storia e destino* [*History and Destiny*] (Turin: Einaudi, 2007) and *Eguaglianza. Una nuova visione sul filo della storia* (Turin: Einaudi, 2019), English edition forthcoming in 2022 (Cambridge, MA: Harvard University Press).

In the case of works cited by the author in Italian translation it wasn't possible to provide page numbers for the original editions.

[1] Walter Benjamin, *Illuminations*, translated by Harry Zohn (New York: Harcourt Brace & World, 1968/Schocken paperback, 1969). Über den Begriff der Geschichte, in W. Benjamin, *Werke und Nachlass*, edited by G. Raulet (Berlin: Suhrkamp, 2010), vol. 19. Zygmunt Bauman recently chose to begin a book with the same text—*Retrotopia* (Cambridge: Polity Press, 2017)—but he uses it in a completely different way from me.

[2] Ernst Bloch, *Verfremdungen* II. *Geographica*, Suhrkamp Verlag, Frankfurt 1964.

[3] Bloch, *Differenzierungen im Begriff Fortschritt*, in Sitzungsberichte der Deutschen Akademie der Wissenschaften zu Berlin, phil. Kl., 5, 1955; and also *Sul progresso*, edited by L. Sichirollo (Milan: Guerini e Associati, 2015).

[4] *Eguaglianza*, cit., pp. 76 ff.

[5] Santo Mazzarino, *Il pensiero storico classico* [*Historical Classical Thought*] vol. II, 2, pp. 412-461 (Bari: Laterza, 1966), (note 555, *L'intuizione del tempo nella storiografia classica* [The intuition of time in classical historiography]). See also: Gennaro Sasso, *Il progresso e la morte. Saggi su Lucrezio* [*Progress and Death. Essays on Lucretius*]

(Bologna: Il Mulino, 1979), especially pp. 163 ff., and Reinhart Kosellek-Christian Meier, *Fortschritt*, in *Geschictliche Grundbegriffe. Historisches Lexicon zur politisch-sozialen Sprache in Deutschland*, vol. II (Stuttgart, Klett-Cotta Verlag, 1975).

⁶ Thomas Burnett, *Telluris Theoria Sacra* (London: 1680), vol. I; trans. *The Sacred Theory of the Earth: Containing an Account of the Original of the Earth and all the General Changes which it hath already undergone, or is to undergo, till the Consummation of All Things*, p. 257 (London, 1691).

⁷ James Hutton, *Theory of the Earth with Proofs and Illustrations*, Edinburgh, William Creech, 1795, vols. I-III. Regarding him, as well as Burnett, see Steven J. Gould's wonderful *Time's Arrow, Time's Cycle. Myth and Metaphor in the Discovery of Geological Time* (Cambridge, MA.-London: Harvard University Press, 1987).

⁸ Voltaire *Essai sur les moeurs et l'esprit des nations et sur les principaux faits de l'histoire, depuis Charlemagne jusqu'à Louis XIII* (Genève: Cramer, 1756).

⁹ Edward Gibbon, *The History of the Decline and Fall of the Roman Empire* (1776), vol. I, p. 78, edited by J.B. Bury (London: Methuen & Co., 1896).

¹⁰ Madame de Staël, *De la littérature considerée dans ses rapports avec les institutions sociales* (Paris: Charpentier, 1800).

¹¹ Jacques Le Goff, "Progresso/reazione," in *Enciclopedia*, edited by R. Romano, vol. XI, p. 213 (Turin: Einaudi, 1980).

¹² F.P.G. Guizot, *Cours d'histoire moderne*, vol. I, *Histoire générale de la civilisation en Europe* (Paris: Pichon et Didier, 1829).

¹³ "Vernunft ist gegenwärtig": thus in a quick note that K. H. Ilting attributes to the 1824-25 lectures in his edition of the *Vorlesungen über Rechtsphilosophie 1818-1831, Edition und Kommentar in sechs Bänden* vol. II, p. 95 (Stuttgart-Bad Cannstatt: Frommann-Holzboog, 1973-74).

¹⁴ Karl Marx, *Einleitung*, in *Zur Kritik der Politischen Ökonomie*, p. 235 (Berlin: Dietz Verlag, 1974). *A Contribution to the Critique of Political Economy*, translated by S. W. Ryazanskaya (Moscow: Progress Publishers, 1970).

¹⁵ Auguste Comte, *Cours de philosophie positive*, vols. I-VI (Paris-Bruxelles: Rouen Frères, 1830-1842).

¹⁶ Pierre-Joseph Proudhon, *Philosophie du progrès. Programme* (Bruxelles: Alphonse Lèbegue, 1853).

¹⁷ Herbert Spencer, *Principles of Psychology* (London: Longman, Brown, Green and Longmans, 1855).

[18] Charles Darwin, *On the Origin of Species by Means of Natural Selection, or the Preservation of Favoured Races in the Struggle for Life* (1859), 6th ed. (London: John Murray, 1872).

[19] David Landes, *The Unbound Prometheus. Technological Change and Industrial Development in Western Europe from 1750 to the Present* (Cambridge: Cambridge University Press, 1969).

[20] The quotation is from J. B. Bury, *The Idea of Progress. An Inquiry into its Origin and Growth* (London: Macmillan, 1920).

[21] Comte, *Discours préliminaire sur l'ensemble du positivisme* (Paris: Mathias, 1848).

[22] Alexis de Tocqueville, *De la démocratie en Amérique* (1840), vol. II, in *Œuvres*, edited by A. Jardin (Paris: Gallimard, 1992) vol. II, p. 544. *Democracy in America*, vol II, translated by Arthur Goldhammer (New York: Library of America, 2004).

[23] Colin Clark, *Conditions of Economic Progress* (London: Macmillan & Co., 1940). See also: Gennaro Sasso, *Tramonto di un mito. L'idea di "progresso" fra Ottocento e Novecento* [*Sunset of a Myth. The idea of "progress" in the eighteenth and nineteenth centuries*] especially pp. 9 ff. and 109 ff. (Bologna: Il Mulino, 1984).

[24] See M. Biscuso, *Nietzsche e il pessimismo di Leopardi* [*Nietzsche and the Pessimism of Leopardi*], in *Filosofia italiana* 12, 2017.

[25] Arthur de Gobineau, *Essai sur l'inégalité des races humaines* 2nd ed., 2 vols. (Paris: Fermin Didot, 1884). *Essay on the Inequality of Human Races*, translated by Adrian Collins (London: William Heinemann, 1915).

[26] *Epistula Encyclica data die VIII decembris MDCCCLIV ad omnes catholicos antistites unacum Syllabo praecipuorum aetatis nostrae errorum* (Ratisbonae: Typis Friderici Pustet, 1865).The encyclical referred to in the title is the Quanta Cura, promulgated along with the Syllabus. The proposition cited is the eightieth, in the tenth section, devoted to "errors having reference to modern liberalism."

[27] *Storia e destino*, cit., pp. 48 ff.

[28] Georges Friedmann, *La crise du progrès. Esquisse d'histoire des idées: 1895-1935* (Paris: Gallimard, 1936).

[29] Georges Sorel, *Les illusions du progrès* (Paris: Rivière, 1908).

[30] Raymond Aron, *Les désillusions du progrès. Essai sur la dialectique de la modernité* (Paris: Calmann-Lévy, 1969).

[31] Bury, *The Idea of Progress*, cit.

[32] "La ginestra" ("Broom"), l. 51, in *Canti*, in *Tutte le opere di Giacomo Leopardi*, 6th ed., edited by F. Flora (Milan: Mondadori, 1958), vol. I, p. 120 (and on this line, in the Notes, p. 142, Leopardi

comments: "Parole di un moderno, al quale è dovuta tutta la loro eleganza" ("Words of a modern, which explains all their elegance"). In *Canti*, translated by Jonathan Galassi (New York: Farrar, Straus & Giroux, 2010).

[33] Eric Hobsbawm, *Ages of Extremes. The Short Twentieth Century, 1914-1991* (London: Penguin Books, 1994).

[34] François Furet, *Le passé d'une illusion. Essai sur l'idée communiste au XX siècle* (Paris: Robert Laffont/Calmann-Lévy, 1995). *The Passing of an Illusion*, translated by Deborah Furet (Chicago: University of Chicago Press, 1999). The title is an obvious reference to Freud's *Die Zukunft einer Illusion* (*The Future of an Illusion*), of 1927.

II WHERE THE ARROW GOES

[35] *Storia e destino*, cit. pp. 23 ff.

[36] Thomas Hobbes, *Leviathan* (1651).

[37] The expression is taken from J. L. Arsuaga, *El collar del Neandertal* (Madrid: Temas de Hoy, 1999). *The Neanderthal's Necklace: In Search of the First Thinkers,* translated by Andy Klatt (New York: Four Walls Eight Windows, 2002). See also *Storia e destino*, cit. pp. 30 ff., p. 103.

[38] The expression is from John McPhee, used in *Basin and Range* (New York: Farrar, Straus & Giroux, 1981); see also Henry Gee, *Deep Time. Cladistics, the Revolution in Evolution* (London: Fourth Estate, 1999). Another fine book is D. Lord Smail, *On Deep History and the Brain* (Berkeley-Los Angeles-London: University of California Press, 2008), in part. pp. 12 ff., 190 ff.

[39] From Stephen J. Gould, in *Wonderful Life. The Burgess Shale and the Nature of History* (New York: Norton, 1989).

[40] Ibid.

[41] Ibid. See also Gould's essay collection *I Have Landed. The End of a Beginning in Natural History*, pp. 29 ff., 241 ff. (New York: Harmony Books, 2002).

[42] I take it again from Gould, *Wonderful Life*, cit.

[43] I take up and modify a formulation that I proposed in *Minima Theoretica*, in A. Romano and S. Sebastiani (editors), *La forza delle incertezze. Dialoghi storiografici con Jacques Revel* [*The force of uncertainty. Historiographical dialogues with Jacques Revel*] (Bologna: Il Mulino, 2016), pp. 71 ff., in part. pp. 78 ff. Based on Stephen Hawking

and Leonard Mlodinow, *The Grand Design* (New York-London: Bantam Books, 2010).

⁴⁴ Jacques Monod, *Le hazard et la nécessité. Essai sur la philosophie naturelle de la biologie moderne,* pp. 19 ff. (Paris: Editions du Seuil, 1970).

⁴⁵ The example is in Roberto Marchesini, *Post-human. Verso nuovi modelli di esistenza* (Turin: Bollati Boringhieri, 2002), pp. 31 ff. (A fine book, but it has the wrong title: the human beyond the species is not "post-human" but simply "post-natural." Why in the world should the "human" be identified only with the "natural"?)

⁴⁶ Thus Jürgen Habermas, *Die Zukunft der menschlichen Natur. Auf dem Weg zu einer liberalen Eugenik?* (Frankfurt am Main: Suhrkamp, 2001). *The Future of Human Nature* (Cambridge: Polity Press, 2003).

⁴⁷ Thus E. O. Wilson, *Consilience. The Unity of Knowledge* (New York: Vintage Books, 1998), pp. 301 ff.—an intelligent book, though with many mistakes and superficialities—cited by Ray Kurzweil, *The Singularity is Near. When Humans Transcend Biology* (New York: Viking Penguin, 2005), p. 195.

⁴⁸ *De antiquissima Italorum sapientia* (1710), in G. Vico, *Metafisica e metodo,* edited by C. Faschilli, C. Greco, and A. Murari (Milan: Bompiani, 2008), ch. I, pp. 194 ff. *On the Most Ancient Wisdom of the Italians: Drawn Out from the Origins of the Latin Language*, translated by J. Taylor (New Haven: Yale University Press, 2010).

⁴⁹ Charles Darwin, *The Descent of Man and Selection in Relation to Sex* (London: Murray, 1871). Also referenced in Marchesini, *Post-human*, cit. pp. 11 ff.

III THE FUTURE FOUND AGAIN

⁵⁰ *Storia e destino* [*History and Destiny*] pp. 78 ff. (Turin: Einaudi, 2007).

⁵¹ Martin Rees, *Our Final Century. Will the Human Race Survive the 21st Century?* (London: Heinemann, 2003).

⁵² I would refer to my *The End of the Past. Ancient Rome and the Modern West,* pp. 204 ff. (Cambridge: Harvard University Press, 2000, repr. 2002). *La storia spezzata. Roma antica e Occidente moderno* (Rome-Bari: Laterza, 1996; new ed. Turin: Einaudi, 2020).

⁵³ Bruno Snell, *Die Entdeckung des Geistes. Studien zur Entstehung des europaischen Denkens bei den Griechen* (Hamburg: Claassen & Goverts, 1955). *The Discovery of the Mind: The Greek*

Origins of European Thought translated by T. G. Rosenmeyer
(Oxford: Blackwell, 1953). See also Jean-Pierre Vernant, *Mythe et
pensée chez les Grecs*, 3rd ed. (Paris: La Découverte, 1990). *Myth and
Thought Among the Greeks*, translated by Jeff Fort (Princeton: Zone
Books, 2006).

[54] Aristotle, *Politics*, 1.2, 1252b. Translated by H. Rackham (Loeb
Classical Library, Cambridge, MA: Harvard University Press, 1944).
Eguaglianza, cit., pp30 ff.

[55] Thus in a fragment of Heraclitus: *Die Fragmente der Vorsokratiker*, ed. Diels-Kranz, 22B F 123; Giorgio Colli, *La natura ama
nascondersi [Nature Loves to Hide]* 2nd ed. (Milan: Adelphi, 1988): a
book of great fascination, even if one can't always agree with it.

[56] Again Heraclitus, *Die Fragmente der Vorsokratiker*, cit., 22B F
101.

[57] I'm thinking of *Politics*, 1.1-2, 1252a-1255b; *Eguaglianza*, cit.
pp. 24 ff.

[58] *The End of the Past*, cit., pp. 108 ff., 175 ff.

[59] Aristotle, *Politics*, cit. 1, 1-2, 1252a-1255b; *Eguaglianza*, cit., pp.
24 ff.

[60] *Eguaglianza*, cit., pp. 32 ff., 63 ff., 68 ff.

[61] As we read on the title page of Sebastiano Serlio's *Quinto Libro
D'Architettura*, published in Paris in 1547, and then in Venice in
1551; Michael Greenhalgh, *Ipsa ruina docet: l'uso dell'antico nel
Medioevo*, in S. Settis (editor), *Memoria dell'antico nell'arte italiana*
(Turin: Einaudi, 1984), vol. I, pp. 113 ff. Also a work of mine: *Il
mondo tardoantico*, in C. Fumian et al., *Storia Medievale* (Roma:
Donzelli, 1998), pp. 43 ff.

[62] *Eguaglianza*, cit., pp. 250 ff.

[63] Ibid., pp. 76 f., 230 ff., 271 ff.

[64] By Gustavo Zagrebelsky, in a public debate with the author of
this book, held in Turin at the Circolo dei Lettori, January 21, 2020.

[65] François Furet, *Penser la Révolution Française* (Paris:
Gallimard, 1985), pp. 51 ff. *Eguaglianza*, cit., pp. 143 ff.

[66] See *la Repubblica*, January 23, 2020, pp. 30 ff. Also keep in
mind Miguel Benasayag's *Organismes et artefacts. Vers la virtualisa-
tion du vivant?* (Paris: La Découverte, 2010), in part. pp. 7 ff., 13 ff.,
85 ff. See also U. Beck, *Weltrisikogesellschaft. Auf der Sache nach der
verlorenen Sicherheit*, Frankfurt am Main: 2007.

[67] *Storia e destino*, cit., pp. 81 ff.

[68] *Eguaglianza,* cit., pp. 281 ff.

[69] See T. Pievani, *Homo sapiens e altre catastrofi. Per un'archeologia

della globalizzazione, 2a ed., Roma, Maltemi, 2006, in part. pp. 29 ff., 247 ff., 340 ff. (an important book); Francis Fukuyama, *Our Posthuman Future. Consequences of the Biotechnology Revolution* (New York: Farrar, Straus & Giroux, 2002); Roberto Marchesini, *Posthuman. Verso nuovi modelli di esistenza*, cit., in part. pp. 72 ff. and also Id., *Il tramonto dell'uomo. Le prospettive post-umaniste* (Bari: Dedalo, 2009), in part. pp. 27 ss., 87 ss.; Michael Frayn, *The Human Touch. Our Part in the Creation of a Universe* (London: Faber & Faber, 2006), in part. pp. 39 ff., 219 ff.; M. Atlan and R.-P. Droit (editors), *Human. Une enquête philosophique sur ces révolutions qui changent nos vies* (Paris: Flammarion, 2012), in part. pp. 39 ff., 100 ff., 419 ff., 477 ff.; G. Pacchioni, *L'ultimo sapiens. Viaggio al termine della nostra specie* (Bologna: Il Mulino, 2019), in part. pp. 29 ff., 181 ff. Also deserving of great attention: Zygmunt Bauman, *Retrotopia* (Cambridge: Polity Press, 2017).

[70] A statement from the celebrated Incipit of the *Confessions* of St. Augustine, I,1.

About the Author

Aldo Schiavone is one of Italy's most renowned historians. He has taught Roman law at the University of Florence and is a member of the American Academy of Arts and Sciences and of Princeton's Institute for Advanced Study. His previous books include *Spartacus* (2013), *Pontius Pilate* (2017) and *The End of the Past* (2000).